The Compassionate Satirist

SOUTH ATLANTIC
MODERN LANGUAGE ASSOCIATION
AWARD STUDY

The Compassionate Satirist

Ben Jonson and His Imperfect World

J. A. Bryant, Jr.

UNIVERSITY OF GEORGIA PRESS

ATHENS

Library of Congress Catalog Card Number: 73–81623
International Standard Book Number: 0–8203–0316–X
The University of Georgia Press, Athens 30602
Copyright © 1972 by the University of Georgia Press
Printed in the United States of America

FOR

Mary Virginia

Contents

Acknowledgments

Anyone in these days who presumes to write about Ben Jonson will unavoidably become indebted to a host of critics and scholars who during the past fifty years have produced a great amount of material dealing with that playwright, his theater, and his times. The names of a number of these appear either in the text of this study or in the notes, and I am grateful to all of them even when on occasion I have felt bound to disagree with some of their views. I am equally grateful, however, to many, many more unnamed here, whose labors have erected the base upon which this and other studies of Ben Jonson must rest.

Like most modern students of Jonson I consider my greatest scholarly creditors to be C. H. Herford and Percy and Evelyn Simpson, from whose monumental *Ben Jonson* in eleven volumes the Clarendon Press has generously permitted me to take my quotations from Jonson's plays. I am also deeply grateful to the editors of *Renaissance Papers*, a publication of the Southeastern Renaissance Conference, and of *Ball State University Forum* for permission respectively to reprint (in revised form) my last chapter, dealing with *A Tale of a Tub*, and a portion of chapter 2 which originally appeared as "Jonson's Satirist Out of His Humor."

CHAPTER ONE

The Scope of the Inquiry

or a long time literary historians have dealt with Ben Jonson's career as if it described in its progress something like an arch or a rainbow. The standard account still begins with Jonson's early imitations of the fashionable mode of Italianate intrigue comedy, *The Case Is Altered* and *Every Man in His Humor*, considers briefly his experiments in comical satire and tragedy, then continues with a more detailed review of his transcendence of all these in four comedies of unmistakable genius and a series of bright masques, and concludes with an apology for Jonson's decline in vigor after 1616 and his eventual return to imitativeness. The revaluation of Jonson's dramatic work that has been under way now for almost half a century has caused changes in the details of the traditional account, though not in the general contour of it. The early comedies no longer seem either so classical or so imitative as they once did. The humor theory has diminished in importance, and the comical satires and tragedies have received more attention. *Volpone* and *The Alchemist* have held their positions of eminence, while *Epicene* and *Bartholomew Fair* have at last begun to come into their own. Some scholars are now even demonstrating that the last plays are not "dotages," as one of the characters in Dryden's *An Essay of Dramatic Poesy* called them, but important embodiments of Jonson's deepest beliefs about the nature and purpose of poetry.[1] During recent years an important concern in Jonson studies has been the tone of the dramatic work—the attitude of the poet toward his characters and the play-world he has created for them, and the relation of both of these to the world outside that Jonson occasionally criticized with memorable asperity. This study is a product of that concern; and although it deals at some length with the earlier work, especially *Every Man in His Humor* and the three comical satires, it gives most attention to *Volpone, Epicene, The Alchemist,* and *Bartholomew Fair.*

In the chapters ahead we shall naturally encounter a fair number of secondary problems, among them the question of the proper dénouement for *Every Man out of His Humor*, the relation among the three Roman poets depicted in *Poetaster* and the values each represents, the function of the comic subplot in *Volpone*, and the use that Jonson made of his machinator-figure in *Epicene* and *The Alchemist*. A major subject of attention in most of the chapters will be the recurring reflections of Jonson's concern over his own role as a public comic poet. There is evidence to suggest that, for those years between 1598 and 1614 when his production for the public theaters was at its richest, he used his dramatic writing partly as a means of understanding the relation of a dramatic poet to society. That is, in the plays themselves he regularly dramatized, both singly and in a variety of permutations and combinations, the public roles that he saw the poet as being obligated to assume from time to time—specifically those of moralist, literary critic, and satirist. He did this with a persistency, moreover, that almost compels one to believe that, as he came to consider himself committed to such obligations, he consciously attempted to explore them in the plays he was writing. In any case this book is in part an attempt to chart Jonson's growth in an area of knowledge that for him most likely became self-knowledge. The charting begins in the present chapter with a review of some of his public pronouncements and an examination of his treatment of morality and poetry in the first version of *Every Man in His Humor*. Thereafter it continues in subsequent chapters with considerations of what appear to be Jonson's successive attempts to deal with other facets of the same problem in the fables of *Volpone*, *Epicene*, *The Alchemist*, and *Bartholomew Fair*. Finally, in all the chapters we shall be deeply concerned with the tone of Jonson's work and the changing vision of life that emerges as we pass from the brilliant early work into the major pieces of his artistic maturity.

With regard to this last matter recent criticism has been divided. An older view that Jonson grew steadily more tolerant as he approached the climax of his career in *Bartholomew Fair* finds expression in Jonas A. Barish's study *Ben Jonson and the Language of Prose Comedy*;[2] but increasingly during the last two decades we have seen in other critical studies evidence of a severer Jonson, one whose attitude toward the world became more jaundiced as he became more successful. For example, Edward B. Partridge, who has written extensively and brilliantly about *Volpone*, *Epicene*, and *The Alchemist*, observes, "We see in his plays the underside of one of the favourite dreams of the Renaissance—the dream of the Golden Age. ... Even as Marlowe dramatized the glamour, the aspirations, and some of the dangers of the Elizabethan Age, so Jonson dramatized the aftermath that could never be more than ideal."[3] Partridge anticipates here the position taken in an even more recent study by Gabriele Bernhard

Jackson, who writes, "The conflict between the glory of what ought to be and the mundane reality of what could be was inherent in his satiric position, but he struggled against its revelation to the end. His later work suffers from the attempt to impose optimism on a world clearly seen by cynical eyes."[4] In Jackson's view Jonson was a reluctant cynic and never gave up struggling to reconcile his compulsion to depict honestly the human race's failure to reach perfection with his stubbornly held vision of a mankind godlike in potential and living under a plan that was originally divine.[5] A briefer but more explicit presentation of Jonson as the congenital satirist is that by Robert Ornstein, who suggests that the explanation for Jonson's pessimistic view, conspicuous even in plays like *Bartholomew Fair*, is his habitual focus: "His comic actions merely disclose the impossibility of transformation in lives that are wholly momentary, compelled by appetite, obsessed by fantasies, untouched by memories or chastened by regret." Moreover, Ornstein represents the playwright as implicitly declaring in *Bartholomew Fair*, "What a piece of work is a man that he should judge his fellows—hog in appetite, fox in stealth, dog in madness, wasp in anger, blind hypocritical fool: Adam, flesh and blood."[6] *Bartholomew Fair*, he observes, might well be considered Ben Jonson's *King Lear*.

Other equally sober views appear here and there in current Jonson criticism; and in the chapters that follow we shall be considering several of them. The corrective that they have provided for older, more simplistic views of Jonson has been salutary on the whole, and the present study is not offered as an absolute contradiction to any of them. Above all it is not intended to obscure what several of these studies, particularly those by Partridge and Jackson, have brought into focus: the ambiguity that characterizes Jonson's more memorable figures and in general his portrayals of life, manners, and morals.

4

This book will present evidence and interpretations of evidence, however, that suggest a less dispiriting view of Jonson's development. Jonson was never a sunny man, and he spent a good part of his life attempting to depict with honesty specimens of the complex human race. To have ended in pessimism would have been the understandable consequence for one who found the corruption, meanness, and villainy that he uncovered and placed on view; but Jonson also found reassuring things in mankind, and some of these seem to have become clear to him only in the course of his activity of re-creating human characters and developing actions for them to come to life in. These we shall be examining at length.

A number of things also will be said about Jonson's artistic principles in the course of this study; but two points, already mentioned in passing in the first paragraph, should be dealt with briefly here at the outset, if only to get them out of the way. First, as regards Jonson's direct imitation of classical works and conventions, that matter seems to have ceased to be an active concern with him early in his development.[7] The statement in *Every Man out of His Humor*, given to the character Cordatus, is as follows:

> I can discerne no such necessity [that is, to obey the laws of comic form]. . . . If those lawes you speake of, had beene deliuered vs, *ab initio*, and in their present vertue and perfection, there had beene some reason of obeying their powers: but 'tis extant, that that which we call *Comœdia*, was at first nothing but a simple, and continued *Song*, sung by one only person. ... [Then down through the time of Aristophanes] euery man in the dignitie of his spirit and iudgement, supplyed something. And (though that in him this kinde of *Poeme* appeared absolute, and fully perfected) yet how is the face of it chang'd since, in MENANDER, PHILEMON, CECILIVS, PLAVTVS, and the rest; who haue vtterly excluded the *Chorus*, altered the prop-

5

erty of the persons, their names, and natures, and augmented it with all liberty, according to the elegancie and disposition of those times, wherein they wrote: I see not then, but we should enioy the same licence, or free power, to illustrate and heighten our inuention as they did; and not bee tyed to those strict and regular formes, which the nicenesse of a few (who are nothing but forme) would thrust vpon vs. (Induction, ll. 245–270)[8]

Although written for a performance in 1599, this assertion of "licence, or free power" remains authentic Jonsonian doctrine for most of his career. After 1599 he seems to have regarded himself consistently as a reincarnation of whatever artistic spirit it was that had animated those ancient authors whom he admired—an act of presumption which irritated some of his contemporaries and too often has intimidated readers in our own time. The important thing about Jonson's body of work, however, is that it represents the activity of a man who combined a knowledgeable scholar's respect for the achievements of the ancients with genius equal to theirs, but who never for a moment forgot that all works of art represent a unique conjunction of independent, living matter with a creator's impulse to order and control. Jonson's work is thus frequently reminiscent of the ancient examples of order that crowded his mind, but his plays are distinctively his and servilely like no others, ancient or modern.

As for the humor theory, that has tended to drop out of sight in recent years. Jonson's significant statement about it also is in the Induction to *Every Man out of His Humor.* There he has the character Asper refer contemptuously to the popular misapplication of the term *humor* to passing fads and affectation and define a true humor as something physiologically determined:

6

> . . . in euery humane body
> The choller, melancholy, flegme, and bloud,
> By reason that they flow continually
> In some one part, and are not continent,
> Receiue the name of Humours. Now thus farre
> It may, by *Metaphore*, apply it selfe
> Vnto the generall disposition:
> As when some one peculiar quality
> Doth so possesse a man, that it doth draw
> All his affects, his spirits, and his powers,
> In their confluctions, all to runne one way,
> This may be truly said to be a Humour.
>
> (Induction, ll. 98–109)

This easy formula by which Jonson explains character in the most pedantic of his popular plays has given rise to a great deal of scholarly discussion about humor in all the others; but, except for an occasional specimen of abnormal psychology like the character Morose in *Epicene*, the whole matter is of negligible importance to an understanding of the plays that Jonson wrote after 1599. Jonson's characterization continued to be soundly based in physiology, at least through *Bartholomew Fair*. The figures in his plays generally are physically memorable and have constitutions appropriate to what they do. This, however, is simply to say that Jonson's genius for comedy from the start tended to be of the naturalistic or earthbound kind, and we shall find that he matured rapidly as soon as he recognized as much and acknowledged his proper medium without misgivings or embarrassment.[9]

It is thus especially interesting to notice that Jonson's first important statement about the nature of poetry is a version of the stereotyped Neo-Platonic justification for "divine Poesy." This occurs in a speech given to the hero of the Quarto version of *Every Man in His Humor,* performed in 1598 and published in 1601. The circumstances leading up to the statement are these. In the fifth act young Lorenzo achieves the conventional victory over his antagonists. With the help of the traditional faithful friend and the equally traditional faithful but mischievous servant he has captured the young woman of his choice; and in spite of the fears of an old-fashioned father he has also proved himself a sober, virtuous, and intelligent exception amidst a society of assorted fools, one of whom is a ridiculously serious poetaster named Matheo. Thus reinstated in everybody's good graces, he is in a good position to intervene when Justice Clement, the deus ex machina of the piece, delivers a well-deserved rebuke to the poetaster and Lorenzo's father takes that opportunity to make a sweeping condemnation of all poetry. Lorenzo's quick rejoinder is a set piece of more than thirty lines, the principal parts of which are as follows:

> I can refell [disprove] opinion, and approue
> The state of poesie, such as it is,
> Blessed, aeternall, and most true deuine:
> . . . .
> ... view her in her glorious ornaments,
> Attired in the maiestie of arte,
> Set high in spirite with the precious taste
> Of sweete philosophie, and which is most,
> Crownd with the rich traditions of a soule,
> That hates to haue her dignitie prophand,
> With any relish of an earthly thought:
> Oh then how proud a presence doth she beare.
> Then is she like her selfe, fit to be seene
> Of none but graue and consecrated eyes:
> Nor is it any blemish to her fame,

8

That such leane, ignorant, and blasted wits,
Such brainlesse guls, should vtter their stolne wares
With such aplauses in our vulgar eares:
Or that their slubberd lines haue currant passe,
From the fat iudgements of the multitude,
But that this barren and infected age,
Should set no difference twixt these empty spirits,
And a true Poet; then which reuerend name,
Nothing can more adorne humanitie.

(v.iii.315–343)

Clement promptly acknowledges the validity of these senti-
ments; hence one supposes that Jonson was willing to let them
pass as a statement of his own view at that point in his career.
The whole speech, however, is an excrescence on an otherwise admirably constructed comedy, and Jonson omitted it
when he revised *Every Man in His Humor* at some time
before 1616. It must have pained him in those later years to
read again the extravagant presentation of his youthful opin-
ions, especially the lines "Crownd with the rich traditions of
a soule, / That hates to haue her dignities prophand, / With
any relish of an earthly thought." In any case, the mature Jonson let Justice Clement respond to the righteously indignant
parent's attack on poetry as follows:

Nay, no speech, or act of mine be drawne against such as
professe it worthily. They are not borne euerie yeere, as an
Alderman. There goes more to the making of a good *Poet*
than a Sheriffe. . . . I will doe more reuerence, to him, when
I meet him, then I will to the Maior, out of his yeere. But,
these paper-pedlers! these inke-dablers! They cannot expect
reprehension, or reproch. They haue it with the fact. (v.v.37–
45)

9

And to this simple but vigorous assertion, the young man of the 1616 version, now called Edward Knowell, replies with, "Sir, you haue sau'd me the labour of a defence."

In the rejected speech, however, there were also ample traces of the essentially Horatian direction that Jonson's mature thinking about poetry was to take. Lorenzo's references to "blasted wits," "brainlesse guls," and "this barren and infected age" suggest that his motive as poet was always at least partly judicial and corrective, and *Every Man in His Humor* as a whole is clearly designed to teach lessons about earthly things and values as well as to amuse. Moreover, by the following year (1599), Jonson had embarked on his series of experiments in comical satire, from which the shadow of Horace was never absent. *Every Man out of His Humor* came out in late fall of that year, *Cynthia's Revels* appeared in 1600, and *Poetaster* in 1601; and all three of these were in a real sense essays in criticism as well as plays. As it turned out, they provided the anvil on which Jonson hammered out the principles that he stated with such confidence in the Epistle Dedicatory to *Volpone*, published for the first time in 1608.

The Epistle Dedicatory to *Volpone* is addressed to "The Most Noble and Most Royall Sisters, The Two Famovs Vniversities," to whom Jonson dedicated both himself and his play and then promised a program that must have startled the authorities at Oxford and Cambridge. His critical position was now completely ethical in orientation: "For, if men will impartially, and not à-squint looke toward the offices, and function of a Poet, they will easily conclude to themselues, the impossibility of any mans being the good Poet, without first being a good man" (ll. 21–23). To this good man he assigned the role of tutor general to the rest of mankind, and he declared him to be above criticism:

He that is said to be able to informe yong-men to all good
disciplines, inflame growne-men to all great vertues, keepe
old-men in their best and supreme state, or as they decline to
child-hood, recouer them to their first strength; that comes
forth the interpreter, and arbiter of nature, a teacher of things
diuine, no lesse then humane, a master in manners; and can
alone (or with a few) effect the businesse of mankind: this,
I take him, is not subiect for pride, and ignorance to exercise
their rayling rhetorique vpon. (ll. 23–31)

Jonson, however, acknowledged much truth in the Puritan
charge "that now, especially in *dramatick*, or (as they term it)
stage-*poetry*, nothing but ribaldry, profanation, blasphemy,
all license of offence to god and man is practis'd" (ll. 35–38);
and with this acknowledgment he put himself, at least as far
as poetry and the theater were concerned, in the role of satirist.
Thus he announced in ringing terms his intention to effect
single-handedly a reformation: "if my MVSES be true to me,
I shall raise the despis'd head of *poetrie* againe, and stripping
her out of those rotten and base rags, wherwith the Times
haue adulterated her form, restore her to her primitive habit,
feature, and maiesty, and render her worthy to be embraced
and kist, of all the great and master-*spirits* of our world"
(ll. 128–134). One should keep in mind that at this time *Volpone* was sharing the stage at the Globe with such plays as
King Lear and *Macbeth* and that even as Jonson was writing
his epistle, Shakespeare was composing *Antony and Cleopatra*
and possibly preparing a version of *Pericles* for performance.
Jonson fortunately had the grace to add, "But that all are
embarqu'd in this bold aduenture for hell, is a most vnchar-
itable thought, and, vtter'd a more malicious slander."

He also exempted himself: "For my particular, I can (and
from a most cleare conscience) affirme, that I haue euer

trembled to thinke toward the least prophanenesse; haue lothed the vse of such foule, and vn-wash'd baudr'y, as is now made the foode of the scene." This was not strictly true, of course; and beneath Jonson's loud and confident affirmation lay a measure of uneasiness and an awareness of questions unanswered and problems not entirely solved. One of these undoubtedly was the question raised by his public abdication of the seat of comedy only a few years before. The question was probably Jonson's alone; one can hardly believe that his audiences gave much thought to the matter. To Jonson, however, it must have seemed crucial. In concluding one performance of *Poetaster* (1601), he had used a short "Apologetical Dialogue" of some 240 lines; and in this he had let a character called "Author," who may have been played by Jonson himself, declare:

> . . . since the *Comick* Mᴠꜱᴇ
> Hath prou'd so ominous to me, I will trie
> If *Tragœdie* haue a more kind aspect.
> Her fauours in my next I will pursue,
> Where, if I proue the pleasure but of one,
> So he iudicious be; He shall b'alone
> A Theatre vnto me. . . .
>
> (ll. 222–228)

In view of Jonson's abiding conviction, stated in various ways throughout his career, of the comic poet's responsibility to "effect the businesse of mankind," this willingness so early in his career to settle for the fit audience though few suggests a confusion and uncertainty of purpose that hinted at trouble to come. Indeed Robert C. Jones, who has speculated at some length on this matter, suggests that Jonson's ambivalent portrayal of the satirist's battle with the world was symptomatic of a deep-seated ambivalence that had already accounted in part for structural flaws in the comical satires and thereafter would continue to show up in plays and poems, whenever the poet's stance became the subject.[10]

Other questions and problems center on a larger problem, namely the alleged incompatibility between satire and poetry. At the root of the difficulty was Jonson's own flat assertion about the impossibility of anyone's becoming a good poet without first being a good man. Strabo had said something like this about geographers, and Quintilian had said as much about orators.[11] It was the kind of statement by which even the best of writers sometimes betray their professional and personal vanity, but Jonson surely knew that all poets are men and that some very good poets from time to time have lived extremely messy lives. Moreover, his own insistence that he himself had been blameless in his practice as satiric poet further aggravated his difficulty; for two of his more distinguished predecessors in the field of comedy, Aristophanes and Plautus, had produced plays with a full share of "vn-wash'd baudr'y" in them, and this Jonson also knew. Perhaps charges and accusations by other contemporary satiric writers had disturbed and put him on the defensive, yet the more general problem continued to challenge and vex him also. Alvin Kernan in his study on Renaissance satire describes how Jonson in his three comical satires sought to meet his problem by objectifying the satirist as a character in each of the three plays.[12] First, in *Every Man out of His Humor* he tried splitting that character into a despicable satiric presenter named Macilente and a righteously indignant author named Asper. When that device proved cumbersome, he put clean satirists into the next two plays, *Cynthia's Revels* and *Poetaster;* but these were ineffective. Thereafter, according to Kernan, Jonson changed his strategy entirely and created a Menippean kind of satire, one which stresses fable and scene rather than the activity of the satirist himself. This, Kernan says, is why the major plays have no formal satirist in them, though traces of the satirist do remain in such figures as Mosca, Truewit, and Humphrey Waspe. Kernan's suggestions about these plays are among the most useful in modern Jonson criticism, and something like what he describes undoubtedly happened as Jonson went about writing them. One should also note, however, that Jonson in *Every Man in His Humor* (1598) had already introduced a character with the satiric function and that he continued to make significant use of some version of that character in every play that he wrote up to and including *Bartholomew Fair* in 1614. Beginning with *Volpone* all the major comedies may reasonably be called Menippean satire, but each one in a specific way deals with what happens when a person with moral pretensions undertakes to sit in judgment on his fellow human beings.

The Quarto version of *Every Man in His Humor* appeared in 1601. There Jonson's first version of the satiric character is called Guiliano; in the Folio of 1616 he goes by the name of Downright. In both texts he is a dour fellow who stands in constant disapproval of his fun-loving brother, Lorenzo junior (Edward Knowell in 1616), and his friends, and in the Quarto he challenges them as follows: "Sblood, I am not affrayed of you nor them neyther, you must haue your Poets, & your caue-leeres, & your fooles follow you vp and down the citie, and heare they must come to domineere and swagger? sirha, you *Ballad singer*, and *Slops* your fellow there, get you out; get you out; or (by the will of God) Ile cut of your eares, goe to" (III.iv.138–144).[13] In the end *Every Man in His Humor* does not vindicate Giuliano; he is rebuked for excessive indignation and is constrained to break bread with the revellers, who repent and are forgiven. Still Giuliano's point of view is not entirely discredited. The young revellers are indeed time wasters; and for all their pretensions they write no poetry, though the principal one of them, the hero of the piece, as we have seen, speaks something like poetry in his concluding defense of the art as "blessed, eternal, and most true divine."

The consistently striking thing about Giuliano and his successors is that of all the characters in Jonson's plays their tone most nearly resembles that of their creator, who could write in his own person (again in the Epistle Dedicatory to *Volpone*): "The increase of ... lust in liberty, together with the present trade of the stage, in all their misc'line *enter-ludes*, what learned or liberall soule doth not already abhor? where nothing but the filth of the time is vtter'd, and that with such impropriety of phrase, such plenty of *solœcismes*, such dearth of sense, so bold *prolepse's*, so rackt *metaphor's*, with brothelry, able to violate the eare of a pagan, and blasphemy, to turne the bloud of a christian to water" (ll. 86–93). One is tempted at this point to be uncharitable and ask whether this is the voice of that good man behind the poetry of *Volpone*. Could Giuliano-Downright of *Every Man in His Humor*, even granted a suitable infusion of poetic talent, have become a candidate for Jonson's Parnassus? If not, does his failure to qualify perhaps suggest something about the failure of both of the indignant satirists in *Every Man out of His Humor* (for neither, as we shall see later, really succeeds on his own in what he sets out to do) or about the ineffectiveness of the "clean" satirists in *Cynthia's Revels* and *Poetaster*? And if all these dramatic objectifications of the author's satiric function fail, what stronger hope is possible for the author himself, who can pronounce judgment in an epistle dedicatory with such splenetic vigor and, one suspects, relish in the office?

There is, of course, no final answer to questions like these; but the possibility that Jonson himself had begun to ask them at this point is quite real. In subsequent chapters we shall be looking at all Jonson's projections of the critic of manners and morals, beginning with a review of those figures in the comical satires, Asper-Macilente, Crites of *Cynthia's Revels*, and Horace of *Poetaster*. *Volpone*, of course, has no obvious denunciator in it. Mosca has a touch of that function, as Kernan has observed; but then Volpone himself has considerably more than a touch, and yet neither he nor Mosca qualifies for the role. The character who does qualify for it, if only barely, is the relatively pallid Peregrine in the subplot; and we shall be looking at him as he begins mild but slips toward the extravagant indignation that entrapped Macilente-Asper and Giuliano-Downright. After that we shall examine the ambiguous Truewit of *Epicene*, noted in passing by Kernan, Surly of *The Alchemist*, and in *Bartholomew Fair* not one character but two, Humphrey Waspe, whose rage far exceeds any that Downright could muster, and Tom Quarlous, whose fate brings us closer to an answer about Jonson's mature views of the liability of playing satirist. In short, all Jonson's comedies from 1598 to 1614 contain at least one sober critic of manners, morals, and sometimes poetry; and in our examination of the plays we shall consider, among other things, Jonson's continuing exploitation of him.[14] In retrospect that exploitation looks suspiciously like an exploration. One cannot quite shake off the feeling that in presenting successive views of the critic, Jonson was objectifying an aspect of himself and that, indeed, in the end he was as relieved as we perhaps are that this troubled and troublesome character could eventually take his turn at leading the company to that banquet table which symbolizes communion with rejoicing humanity.

If the angry critic comes to the feast only by virtue of a metamorphosis of the indignation that threatened to drive him in the opposite direction, another kind of troublemaker in Jonson's plays, one less inconvenienced by morality, seems to some readers to get there by a principle aptly stated by Justice Clement when he pardons the machinator Brainworm in the revised version of *Every Man in His Humor:* "Thou hast done, or assisted to nothing, in my judgment, but deserues to bee pardon'd for the wit o' the offence. If thy master, or anie man, here, be angrie with thee, I shall suspect his ingine, while I know him for't" (v.iii.112–115). This would appear to be the same hole in the net by which Jeremy-Face of *The Alchemist* and all the Bartholomew birds escape, to the perennial confusion of moralistic critics of Jonson everywhere. One might say that Jonson's moral sense is simply deficient here. Or, one might say that his ethic, perhaps based on a Catholic faith in the essential goodness of the world as it is, required that all such merely playful spirits be forgiven for their innocent mischief—even though nothing in that ethic forbade the condemnation of an earnest reformer with his acute perception of corruption and his motive to check it. In addition one might note also that the Brainworms of this world are akin to the poet in their creativity and in the delight with which they pursue for its own sake their vocation of making; thus Jonson conceivably may have been prejudiced in their favor. The difficulty with these views, particularly the last two, is that Volpone is really a poet in the same sense as Brainworm, and "wit of the offense" does not save him. For that matter neither does it save Mosca, who succeeds Volpone as machinator in the last act of the play. In any case we shall be considering this matter, too, as we proceed through the plays and observe how the problem of the machinator tends to coalesce with the problem of the satirist in that resolution which Jonson's comedy achieves fully only in the smells and dusty heat of Smithfield.

As for the plays that Jonson wrote after *Bartholomew Fair* there is, with one exception and possibly two, little evidence in them of the comic epiphany that Jonson achieved in his masterpiece of 1614. *The Devil Is an Ass,* which came out in 1616, a year of great public triumphs for Jonson, was a clever invention distinguished by some moderately good satire and lyrical passages but otherwise not especially noteworthy; and the stage plays which Jonson is known to have written after 1625 —*The Staple of News, The New Inn,* and *The Magnetic Lady* —are even less interesting from the point of view of this study. These last three plays do not deserve Dryden's epithet "dotages," but their mode is tidiness, and their appeal is to the wit. On going through them one finds a feebler pulse beat along the way and at the end of each only a dénouement. It is almost as if Jonson wrote them in order to give exposition to something that he already understood and not out of any need to know experientially something that he had only dimly perceived with his intellect. For all their finish there is little urgency about these plays, and his audiences found them unexciting.

The exceptions are *The Sad Shepherd* (a fragment) and *A Tale of a Tub.* The second of these possibly belongs to an earlier period, but it was certainly performed near the end of Jonson's life; and it is this play which provides the focus for the final chapter in this book. No apology is needed for letting it stand in company with Jonson's best. Like all his plays *A Tale of a Tub* exhibits the marks of Roman ancestry brought home and completely naturalized, and like his best work it shows beneath these the clear traces of that heritage which Plautus and Terence shared with Aristophanes, rustic man's ritual play and even ritual itself, both containing in their forms a memorial of the primitive's recognition of the wonder and beauty of his world and his celebration of conscious union with it. If *A Tale of a Tub* is Jonson's last play, it preserves in the melancholy period of his decline much of the joy that he was able to generate in the developing action of *Bartholo-mew Fair;* having been performed then, it preserves that joy in any case, regardless of when it was composed. There is no machinator-poet in it, unless one considers the absurd In-and-In Medley of the last act to be cast in that role; and there is no angry critic or satirist anywhere to be seen. Indeed "anger" is a word that does not come up in the discussion of this play in which the attitude toward human folly is one of charitable forbearance. If *A Tale of a Tub* had an early life as well as a late one, as many now seem to believe, then the play shows that Jonson's effective career in the theater came full circle more neatly than some have thought, with a fresh, unsophisticated pursuit of human happiness at the beginning as well as at the end.

CHAPTER TWO

Comical Satire

The Playwright in the Play

he plays that Jonson wrote in the three years immediately following the first version of *Every Man in His Humor* (1598) do not show any deliberate advance toward the more sophisticated structure of the later version of that play or of the *Volpone* that he was to write several years later. In the motto on the title page of *Every Man out of His Humor* (1599) he calls that piece a "comicall satyre," and in the critical induction to the play he has one of the speakers describe it as an innovation, "somewhat like *Vetus Commoedia*" (l. 232), and defend innovation generally as one of the fundamental responsibilities of a true comic writer.[1] Some of the structural innovations of *Every Man out of His Humor*, however, can probably be put down to carelessness. One charitable modern critic has called the play "panoramic,"[2] but most others have thought it simply formless or rambling.[3] The structure of the second of the comical satires, *Cynthia's Revels* (1600), is not particularly distinctive either. It has a curious imbalance among the acts suggestive of the customary division of Shakespeare's *Love's Labor's Lost* and doubtless caused, as in Shakespeare's play, by the need to include a series of entertainments; but apart from that it is conventionally built. The unusual features of *Poetaster* (1601), such as they are, are pretty clearly the result of Jonson's decision to complete the play prematurely and in great haste. In short his announcement in 1599 that he was moving in the direction of "Old Comedy" appears in retrospect to have been more of a request for indulgence than anything else, at least as far as form was concerned. His discovery that structure could be as meaningful as language, beautifully demonstrated in the appropriate shape he worked out for his masterly revision of *Every Man in His Humor*, did not manifest itself in a new play until *Volpone*. Jonson's primary concern here in 1599, fresh as he was with the confidence that his first real success must have brought him, was to work out and present in a new series of plays the appropriate relation between the kind of comic poet he himself could understand and seek to be and the principal subject matter of such a poet, society at large.[4]

In the beginning Jonson probably had no notion of projecting an image of himself and little more than a passing interest in responding to the caricature in John Marston's revision of *Histriomastix*, presented by Paul's Boys earlier that same season.[5] Still, regardless of intention, an author who presents publicly an idealized version of an office that he himself holds or clearly would like to hold lays himself open to the kind of misinterpretation that Jonson received, if it was misinterpretation; and he invites detraction. For all its explicit statement *Every Man out of His Humor* was apparently misunderstood even on that one occasion when the actors presented the play as Jonson first conceived and wrote it. Much of subsequent commentary suggests that it has continued to be misunderstood. *Cynthia's Revels*, which marks no significant advance on any front, was probably never seriously misunderstood by anyone except Jonson himself, though understandably Jonson may have been merely reluctant to acknowledge the vanity that others were quick to see in it. Edmund Wilson has made a case for believing that Jonson was by nature an expressionistic writer who constantly thrust into public view recognizable pieces of his psychic anatomy.[6] If Wilson is only half right, Dekker in his projected *Satiromastix* was taking aim not merely at a Jonsonian ideal dramatically presented but at an authentic and very vulnerable image of Jonson himself as well. In any event, in *Poetaster*, which the Children of the Chapel got into production early in 1601 ahead of *Satiromastix*, Jonson praised himself in the character of Horace and made fun of others, notably Dekker and Marston under the figures of Demetrius and Crispinus. In fairness one must acknowledge that he assigned no views to his Horace which could not plausibly be attributed to the historical Horace and he chastised his detractors with more good humor than malice. The real attack in *Poetaster* was directed against Ovid and the attitude toward poetry assigned to him there, and the greater praise went to Virgil; for neither of these characters was there an identifiable counterpart in Jonson's theatrical circle. In fact *Poetaster* is mainly concerned to praise virtue in a commonwealth and to demonstrate that both poetry and satire have their really significant roles in the public support of such virtue. Thus as a relatively serious play it probably did much to make Jonson's conscious purposes clear and may have hastened the end of all the trivial disputes. Writing that play seems also to have cleared Jonson's own thinking and confirmed in him the self-knowledge that is implicit in his four major comedies and explicit in the Epistle Dedicatory to *Volpone* of 1607.

In the epistle, as we have seen, Jonson declared "the impossibility of any mans being the good Poet, without first being a good man" and then went on to describe a good poet as one who "can alone (or with a few) effect the businesse of man-kind" (ll. 29–30). The qualification "with a few" is perhaps more important than may at first appear. Confident as Jonson must have been of his own integrity as a man and as a poet, he had by this time come to acknowledge one special requirement for the satirist, or indeed for any poet presuming to pass judgment on his fellow man. If a king, as everyone knew, rules only by the grace of God, then a satirist, Jonson was now convinced, rails with impunity only by the grace of his sovereign. Of course, being human and himself, Jonson continued to judge men and their manners in his plays; but after 1607 he tried to judge with more tolerance than he had previously and in greater awareness of what must happen to any fallible human creature who presumes to pass judgment with no higher authority than his own to support him. The poet, he knew, must have someone above him. Moreover the poet must live and work in society as a man; thus he can never be without responsibility, and he can never be self-sufficient. Jonson tried to spell these principles out for himself and his audiences in all the comical satires. He made his most spectacular attempt, however, unfortunately without much success, in the first of the three, *Every Man out of His Humor*.

One reason for the customary neglect of *Every Man out of His Humor* is that the title naturally links it with the more formally constructed *Every Man in His Humor* of 1598, by comparison with which it has been characterized as loose and formless. Another reason is that Jonson's own designation of it as a "comicall satyre" links it in a special way with *Cynthia's Revels* and *Poetaster*, both of which, in addition to being more conventionally planned, contain considerably more of that abusive kind of satire which has made all these plays interesting to historical scholars. Thus there has always been the tendency to let *Every Man out of His Humor* fall between two stools and very little tendency to inquire whether it may not perhaps deserve a stool of its own. A much greater obstacle to appreciation, however, has been the form in which the play has come down to us. When audiences objected to the first ending Jonson wrote for it, he obligingly devised another; and it was this version of *Every Man out of His Humor* that he published in the Quarto of 1600, though he did manage to salvage something of his integrity by appending a note explaining in considerable detail his original intentions.[7] His ending for the Folio version shows still another revision, but one that does not appreciably alter the dénouement of the Quarto version; and neither of these "authorized" endings provides the cap of meaning which the ending that Jonson describes in his note must have provided. As printed, *Every Man out of His Humor* has become a brilliantly written though rambling comical satire embedded in a somewhat wordy dramatic frame, in which a pair of critics do nothing but comment on the various episodes and enunciate Jonson's views of comedy. It ends when Macilente, manipulator of the action and critic of society in the play proper, runs out of fools to expose. As planned and first written, the play is considerably more than that.

Thanks to Jonson's note, it is not difficult to reconstruct the play that he originally conceived and executed. The frame in all the versions begins as two young gentlemen, Cordatus and Mitis, have just seated themselves on the stage to watch a new comedy by their friend Asper, who is also to play the leading role. Asper himself presently steps forth to greet them, roundly denounces the world of fools he has scourged in his script, and then, after a halfhearted greeting to the gathering throng, rushes backstage to get into costume, leaving his friends to talk learnedly about the theory of comedy and the special nature of the play they are about to see. Moments later Asper's play, or the play proper, begins. In that play the central figure is a talented, widely traveled, scholarly but disillusioned person named Macilente, who has the perception to see that the world is a place where fools often fare better than wise men. With respect to the other characters he functions as both presenter and purger, revealing their follies, or "humors," and moving them into situations in which they may receive correction. In both the Quarto and the Folio versions of the play Macilente disposes of the follies of Fallace, Deliro, and Brisk, thus bringing them "out of humor," and then turns to the audience with the following lame comment by way of conclusion:

Why, here's a change! Now is my soule at peace.
I am as emptie of all enuie now,
As they of merit to be enuied at.
My humour (like a flame) no longer lasts
Then it hath stuffe to feed it, and their folly,
Being now rak't vp in their repentant ashes,
Affords no ampler subiect to my spleene.
I am so farre from malicing their states,
That I begin to pitty 'hem. It grieues me
To thinke they haue a being. I could wish
They might turne wise vpon it, and be sau'd now,
So heauen were pleas'd. . . .

(v.xi.54–65)

In the Quarto Jonson goes on for thirty-two more lines, bidding "with *Aspers* tongue (though not his shape)" for the

applause of his audience. In the Folio he breaks off at this
point, lets the chorus reappear briefly to express its satisfaction, and then makes his bid for applause in prose.

The original ending of the play was quite different apparently. In that version Macilente also managed to get everybody out of humor, just as he has continued to do in the
revised versions of Quarto and Folio; but in addition he was
forced to acknowledge that in correcting others he had put
himself in far more desperate need of correction than they had
ever been. Evidence of Jonson's intention in this matter appears in all versions of the play. As early as Act I Macilente
anticipates an ironic outcome for his activity by telling us in a
soliloquy that he cannot safely contemplate the folly of the
miser Sordido because

> . . . he surfets in prosperitie,
> And thou (in enuie of him) gnaw'st thy selfe,
> Peace, foole, get hence, and tell thy vexed spirit,
> "Wealthy in this age will scarcely looke on merit."
>
> (1.iii.84–87)

In a subsequent critical episode Cordatus explains to Mitis:
"You must vnderstand, Signior, he enuies him not as he is a
villaine, a wolfe i' the common-wealth, but as he is rich, and
fortunate; for the true condition of enuie is, *Dolor alienæ
fælicitatis*, to haue our eyes continually fixt vpon another mans
prosperitie, that is, his chiefe happinesse, and to grieue at
that" (1.iii.162–167). As a final direct reminder, Cordatus
interrupts again, at the end of Act IV, to announce that before
the play is over "you shall see the very torrent of his enuie
breake forth like a land-floud" (IV.vii.155–156). In the published versions of the play nothing of the sort happens.

According to Jonson's note, however, the original version

26

of *Every Man out of His Humor* not only fulfilled Cordatus's promise of a "land-floud" stage for Macilente's envy; it also provided a very special correction for it:

> There was nothing (in his [Jonson's] examin'd *Opinion*) that could more neare or truly exemplifie the power and strength of her inualuable *Vertues*, than the working of so perfect a *Miracle* on so oppos'd a *Spirit*, who not only persisted in his *Humor*, but was now come to the *Court* with a purpos'd resolution (his Soule as it were new drest in *Enuie*) to maligne at any thing that should front him; when sodainly (against expectation, and all steele of his *Malice*) the verie wonder of her *Presence* [the Queen's] strikes him to the earth dumbe, and astonisht. From whence rising and recouering heart, his *Passion* thus utters it selfe.[8]

The address to the Queen which followed at this point fortunately was preserved as an appendix in both the Quarto and the Folio. The pertinent lines from it are these:

> Neuer till now did obiect greet mine eyes
> With any light content: but in her graces,
> All my malicious powers haue lost their stings.
> Enuie is fled my soule, at sight of her,
> And shee hath chac'd all black thoughts from my bosome,
> Like as the sunne doth darkenesse from the world.
> My streame of humour is runne out of me.
> And as our cities torrent (bent t' infect
> The hallow'd bowels of the siluer *Thames*)
> Is checkt by strength, and clearnesse of the riuer,
> Till it hath spent it selfe e'ene at the shore;
> So, in the ample, and vnmeasur'd floud
> Of her perfections, are my passions drown'd:
> And I haue now a spirit as sweet, and cleere,
> As the most rarefi'd and subtile aire.[9]

Critics sometimes treat these lines as if they were part of something composed for a special performance at which the Queen herself was expected to be present; yet Jonson's note makes it clear that the address was also an indispensable part of his original conception of Macilente's action as one in which a perceptive critic, having diagnosed and exposed a spiritual plague in others, suddenly finds that he himself is mortally infected. Macilente's grateful words here at the end constitute an acknowledgment that his restoration to sanity has come in the only way really consistent with Ben Jonson's ethic—that is, as a free gift of goodness bestowed vicariously by a sovereign who is himself (or here, herself) manifestly good and divinely sanctioned. Any suggestion that Macilente could have served as his own physician would have been in Jonson's scheme of things an absurdity.

Jonson's alteration of the ending has also made it difficult to see that Asper himself has a serious humor and that his purgation is really the unifying action of the play. For example, Nicholson and Herford in the popular Mermaid edition listed Macilente's name in the dramatis personae as follows: "Macilente (Asper, i.e. B. Jonson 'out of his humour')"; and to Jonson's description of Asper in "The Characters of the Persons" (added by him in the Folio) they attached a note saying that Asper's name means "rough and rugged one" and that he represents Jonson himself as presenter.[10] The implication of both of these notes is that Asper, like the other two members of the "chorus," is not really involved in any action but that he joins with Cordatus and Mitis in presenting an attitude toward folly which Jonson would invite his audiences to share.[11] Obviously the sole function of Cordatus (sound judgment) and Mitis (maturity or ripeness) is to raise and answer questions that might be expected to occur to any intelligent viewer: and since Cordatus gives most of the answers and defends the play, he if anyone is probably "Ben Jonson out of his humor."[12]

Asper's function, however, is quite another matter. The etymological meaning of his Latin name is "without hope," as Jonson undoubtedly was aware; and he represents, not Jonson specifically, but any satirist-author in his role of angry man, consumed with hate for the fools he has created and for their counterparts out in the real world. "With an armed, and reso1ued hand," he says in his first speech, "Ile strip the ragged follies of the time, / Naked, as at their birth" (Induction, ll. 16–18). Mitis and Cordatus, distressed at the violence of their friend's "strong thoughts," urge caution lest he stir the audience to resentment or find himself consumed with his own "humor." It is Mitis's use of this last term that prompts Asper's famous definition. The word *humor*, he points out, is improperly used to refer to foolish pretense or affection. It is correctly applied only to some genuine and deep-seated disturbance in the human psyche,

> As when some one peculiar quality
> Doth so possesse a man, that it doth draw
> All his affects, his spirits, and his powers,
> In their confluctions, all to runne one way,
> This may be truly said to be a Humour.
>
> (Induction, ll. 106–109)

Such a disturbance is not in itself necessarily physiological, but it is analogous to a serious physiological imbalance of the fluids, or humors, in the body; and hence it corresponds pretty closely to what we should today call a neurosis or a psychosis, depending on the severity of it. It also includes Macilente's envy, which a theologian would call sin; and, ironically, it also includes Asper's own neurotic anger, though he himself seems completely unaware of that.

Mitis and Cordatus are aware of it, however, as their protestations in the Induction clearly show; and even though Asper does not return in his own person again until the end of the play, Cordatus reminds us of his predicament in the passage at the conclusion of Act I in which he explains the nature of Macilente's envy: "if we make his [that is, the fool's] monstrous and abhord actions our obiect, the griefe (we take then) comes neerer the nature of hate, then enuie, as being bred out of a kinde of contempt and lothing, in our selues" (I.iii.167–171). In fact, Asper's humor of anger is a thing more to be feared than Macilente's envy, though either should be enough to give a victim cause for grave concern. In the eyes of the Elizabethan psychologist both conditions are potentially deadly; considered from the point of view of a theologian both result from the same kind of prideful presumption and are mortally sinful, differing only in degree and extent of aggravation.

Thus to Cordatus and Mitis, and to all of us who encounter *Every Man out of His Humor* in its first form, the action of the play may be summed up briefly as follows: a satirist (Asper), seeing both the follies of the world and the pitfall of envy that threatens even the righteous man who would presume to correct such things, devises a parable to expose the foolish and warn the wise; yet in so doing he falls victim to his own righteous anger and proves nothing quite so clearly as that he too is human and vulnerable. We see all this unmistakably at the end, when the playwright-actor in the play, still wearing the costume of the character in his dramatic poem but speaking now with his own voice, appears before us to make his conventional bid for applause and inadvertently reveals that all along the worldly wise Macilente, condemned by the play for his envy, has been in addition the projection of an even more desperately infected Asper. The moral for both—and for all ordinary mortals—is nowhere better stated than in the "Judge not, that ye be not judged" of the Sermon on the Mount (Matt. 7:1–2); and the miraculous dispensation is the only kind of happy conclusion that Jonson could have provided for his two arrogant critics, neither of whom could possibly have seen through the pride in his own eye and saved himself. The only other credible conclusion for them would have been some kind of condemnation; but Jonson, having given them grace and forgiveness instead, unfortunately bowed to the wishes of his first audience and contrived modified endings that obscured for subsequent viewers and most readers the means whereby he had originally spared them. Today, however, because he at least insisted on the preservation of Macilente-Asper's address to the Queen in all versions printed during his lifetime, we can arrive, by a modest effort at reconstruction, at the attitude toward satire and satirists that Jonson considered to have been so well established by his first comical satire that he could let it serve as the self-evident basis for his second, *Cynthia's Revels*, in 1600.

In *Cynthia's Revels* we are expected to take for granted the validity of the principles established in *Every Man out of His Humor:* first, the satirist must be a good man, well informed and morally responsible; and, second, he must speak with the authority of someone higher than himself. The first of these principles would probably have seemed self-evident to Jonson's audiences, even without the didacticism of *Every Man out of His Humor*. Shakespeare, writing at about the same time, put that principle into *As You Like It* when he had the banished Duke rebuke Jaques for wanting to put on motley and become a clown like Touchtone. "What, for a counter, would I do but good?" Jaques had asked enthusiastically. The Duke's answer was brief and pointed:

Most mischievous foul sin, in chiding sin.
For thou thyself has been a libertine,
As sensual as the brutish sting itself;
And all th' embossed sores and headed evils
That thou with license of free foot hast caught,
Wouldst thou disgorge into the general world.

(ii.vii.64–69)

Reading on in *As You Like It*, we find at the root of Jaques's libertinism, and indeed at the root of all his restless melancholy, the canker worm of self-love, which is precisely the bane, potential or actual, of all Jonson's satirists. This is the reason for the second principle; no satirist can be serene or efficient unless he can lose himself in dedicated service to some higher power, patron, or sovereign. Here, in presenting explicitly the destructiveness of self-love, *Cynthia's Revels* makes its special contribution to the inquiry of Jonson's comical satires into the nature of satire and the special problems that beset those who practice it.

Jonson begins this play with an illustration of what self-love did to Narcissus, who became in his fate the classic type of that malady; then he proceeds to show—tediously some would say—what self-love can do to a group of irresponsible courtiers, whose only duty presumably is to submerge self in the service of their queen; and finally he shows what self-love came close to doing even to a high-minded scholar-poet, Crites, who briefly but still almost disastrously for his own peace of mind imagined that he stood alone, censuring on his own authority and not as the servant of his sovereign. So that we ourselves may have no excuse for forgetting what the play is all about, Jonson makes his emblematic presentation of the principle, the Narcissus episode, one of the really arresting things in this generally tiresome play.[13]

The episode appears before the play proper has gone through two hundred lines of text. Cupid, rankled because of his proscription by the fickle lords and ladies of Diana's court, has resolved to go among them disguised as a page and take proper revenge with his bow. The prankster god Mercury, to whom he confides his intention, is eager to participate in the joke but says that he must first discharge a special assignment Jove has given to him. He has been commanded to revive the nymph Echo, voiceless and incorporeal now for three thousand years, and give her an opportunity to vent her pent-up grief over the loss of Narcissus, who as we all know fell fatally in love with his own reflection in a fountain. At her awakening, which follows immediately, Echo deplores in her first speech the dilemma that plagues fallible humanity whenever it gains possession of some virtue—goodness, truth, or in this case beauty:

> Why did the gods giue thee a heau'nly forme,
> And earthy thoughts, to make thee proud of it?
> Why, doe I aske? Tis now the knowne disease
> That beautie hath, to beare too deepe a sense
> Of her owne selfe-conceiued excellence.
> O, hadst thou knowne the worth of heau'ns rich gift,
> Thou wouldst haue turn'd it to a truer vse,
> And not (with staru'd, and couetous ignorance)
> Pin'd in continuall eying that bright gem,
> The glance whereof to others had beene more,
> Than to thy famisht mind the wide worlds store. . . .
>
> (1.ii.40–50)

Nothing in Echo's speech is really applicable to the affected Amorphous or the zany Asotus, who in the next two scenes enact a parody on the Narcissus theme; but much of what she says is applicable to the scholar Crites, who brings the scene to a close with a diatribe on the follies of such creatures:

> O how despisde and base a thing is a man,
> If he not striue t'erect his groueling thoughts
> Aboue the straine of flesh! But how more cheape
> When, euen his best and vnderstanding part,
> (The crowne, and strength of all his faculties)
> Floates like a dead drown'd bodie, on the streame
> Of vulgar humour, mixt with commonst dregs?
> I suffer for their guilt now, and my soule
> (Like one that lookes on ill-affected eyes)
> Is hurt with meere intention on their follies.
>
> (I.v.33–42)

This speech of Crites's calls to mind not only Asper from *Every Man out of His Humor*—"Who is so patient of this impious world, / That he can checke his spirit, or reine his tongue?" (Induction, ll. 4–5) and "Ile strip the ragged follies of the time, / Naked, as at their birth" (Induction, ll. 17–18) —but also Asper's unhappy creature Macilente, who observed all the fools round about him and then wailed:

> When I see these (I say) and view my selfe,
> I wish the organs of my sight were crackt;
> And that the engine of my griefe could cast
> Mine eye-balls, like two globes of wild-fire, forth,
> To melt this vnproportion'd frame of nature.
> Oh, they are thoughts that haue transfixt my heart,
> And often (i' the strength of apprehension)
> Made my cold passion stand vpon my face,
> Like drops of dew on a stiffe cake of yce.
>
> (I.i.24–32)

We know what happened to Asper and Macilente; but Crites is presumably superior to these in perception and understanding, and that superiority perhaps accounts for his ability to avoid making the violent responses to folly that his predecessors made. Instead he simply views it with relatively quiet grief. Still, violent or not, the judgment of others involves a standard; and when the standard is self, there is always the danger of self-love—or, to paraphrase Echo, the disease that comes of having too deep a sense of self-conceived excellence.

Of all the characters in the play—or, for that matter, of all the characters in drama—Crites probably has most right to "a deep sense of self-conceived excellence." By definition he is about as close to perfection as a human being can get, and hence as a character who passes judgment on the author's enemies is (or at least he was in the view of Jonson's detractors) a perfect example of Jonsonian self-praise. Mercury, who sees him with the eyes of a god and thus presumably sees correctly, describes Crites in terms that are almost too good to be true; yet they undoubtedly set forth what Jonson at this point in his career regarded as an ideal:

> A creature of a most perfect and diuine temper. One, in whom the humours and elements are peaceably met, without emulation of precedencie: he is neyther to phantastikely melancholy, too slowly phlegmaticke, too lightly sanguine, or too rashly cholericke, but in all, so composde & order'd, as it is cleare, *Nature* went about some ful worke, she did more than make a man, when she made him. His discourse is like his behauiour, vncommon, but not vnpleasing; hee is prodigall of neyther. Hee striues rather to bee that which men call iudicious, then to bee thought so: and is so truly learned, that he affects not to shew it. Hee will thinke, and speake his thought, both freely: but as distant from deprauing another mans merit, as proclaiming his owne. For his valour, tis such, that he dares as

little to offer an inurie, as receiue one. In summe, he hath a
most ingenuous and sweet spirit, a sharp and season'd wit, a
straight iudgment, and a strong mind. *Fortune* could neuer
breake him, nor make him lesse. He counts it his pleasure, to
despise pleasures, and is more delighted with good deeds, then
goods. It is a competencie to him that hee can bee vertuous. He
doth neyther couet, nor feare; hee hath too much reason to doe
eyther: and that commends all things to him. (ii.iii.123–145)

For Crites, in short, virtue is its own reward; and in that
respect he is certainly the richest of mortals. Nevertheless, he
is mortal; and mortality keeps him from being self-sufficient,
regardless of how close he may come to that ideal.

Being as nearly perfect as a mortal can be, he is probably
invulnerable to Macilente's vice of envy; but like Asper he
can know anger, and like any other limited human being he
can come to despair. This is almost what happens to Crites
at the end of Act iii. Two despicable court caterpillars, the
amorist Hedon and impudent Anaides, have been repulsed
by their ladies and lay the blame for their discomfiture on
Crites, who, unknown to them, is listening to all they say.
Hedon is for attacking the scholar with open censure, but
wily Anaides urges that they discreetly spread about the
word that Crites is a confirmed plagiarist. As they leave the
apartment, Crites comes forth and in soliloquy makes it clear
how little he is troubled by any threats these two may make
against him:

> What should I care what euery dor doth buzze
> In credulous eares? it is a crowne to me,
> That the best iudgements can report me wrong'd;
> Them lyars; and their slanders impudent.
> Perhaps (vpon the rumour of their speeches)
> Some grieued friend will whisper to me, CRITES

Men speake ill of thee; so they be ill men,
If they spake worse, 'twere better: for of such
To be disprais'd, is the most perfect praise.
What can his censure hurt me, whom the world
Hath censur'd vile before me?

(iii.iii.8-18)

Soon Lady Arete (virtue) joins him, however, and we quickly
see that Crites is deeply stirred with something like righteous
indignation, as he delivers himself of a satire that runs for
more than eighty lines and rapidly increases in bitterness as
it goes. Finally Arete stops the corrosive effect of Crites's
anger by putting an end to his satire:

Patience, gentle CRITES.
This knot of spiders will be soone dissolu'd,
And all their webs swept out of CYNTHIAS court,
When once her glorious *deitie* appeares,
And but presents it selfe in her full light.

(iii.iv.87-91)

Instead of delivering judgments, she urges, he must

Thinke on some sweet, and choice inuention, now,
Worthie her serious, and illustrous eyes,
That from the merit of it we may take
Desir'd occasion to preferre your worth,
And make your seruice knowne to CYNTHIA.

(iii.iv.95-99)

Crites immediately sees the wisdom of his counsellor's words,
kisses her hands and dedicates himself to her and his Queen.
Thus with Crites's illumination we pass the real crisis, and
the only climax, of *Cynthia's Revels*. All the rest, the exposure
of folly after its addiction to self-love and the public vindica-

37

tion of Crites, is the consequence of this undramatic but thematically important bit of business.

Crites almost learns his lesson too well. After a long Act IV, in which the courtiers all become addicted to self-love and thus render poor Cupid's bow impotent, Crites is asked to provide a court masque to honor Cynthia's return to her throne. At first he declines on the grounds that his queen deserves only something perfect and the materials with which he must work will not admit of perfection:

> Better, and sooner durst I vnder-take
> To make the different seasons of the yeere,
> The windes, or elements to sympathize,
> Then their unmeasurable vanitie
> Dance truely in a measure.
>
> (v.v.4–8)

Arete quickly corrects his error. It is not the business of the poet to produce true harmony, or truth of any sort: the poet can only prepare the way. Cynthia wishes him to do just that.

> There is your error. For as HERMES wand
> Charmes the disorders of tumultous ghosts,
> And as the strife of *Chaos* then did cease,
> When better light then Natures did arriue:
> So, what could neuer in it selfe agree,
> Forgetteth the *eccentrike* propertie,
> And at her sight, turnes forth-with regular,
> Whose scepter guides the flowing *Ocean*.
>
> (v.v.15–22)

Thereafter Crites proceeds to produce a formal masque in which the mortally foolish courtiers present the shapes of those virtues which are the opposite of the very vices by which

they live. Cynthia understands and is pleased, and she promptly and graciously recognizes Crites for the genuine virtue that
exempts him from the gloomy multitude. "Henceforth be
ours," she says, "the more thy selfe to be" (v.viii.35).

Later in the act, when the unmasking has occurred and all
have been revealed for what they are, Arete, or Virtue, dele-
gates to Crites the godlike prerogative of judgment; and
Crites proves his worthiness by judging like a god, dispensing
penance rather than punishment and mercifully seeking reformation for his culprits rather than condemnation. He recognizes, moreover, that he judges by Virtue's permission and
in the name of his sovereign. Cynthia again approves and
pronounces the moral, for satirists and for everybody:

> Princes, that would their people should doe well,
> Must at themselues begin, as at the head;
> For men, by their example, patterne out
> Their imitations, and reguard of lawes:
> A vertuous *Court* a world to vertue drawes.
>
> (v.xi.169–173)

Virtue and the responsibility for virtue, it appears, both begin
at the top.

Poetaster, first produced in 1601, does something different
from either of its immediate predecessors: it deals with satire
as a separate genre (Asper had been a playwright and Crites
simply a scholarly poet in general); and it questions whether
satire, thus ioslated from the more respectable literary forms,
has any right to a permanent place in poetry's pantheon. The
question is basic and makes one wonder whether *Poetaster*
may not actually be the oldest of the three comical satires. In
spite of all the marks of hasty composition, the play appears
on examination to have scaffolding and texture that could

very well have preceded Jonson's involvement in the war of the theaters. It is possible and even likely that adaptation of the play to the details of London's theatrical scene was a last-minute development, made easier by the fact that Ovid, one of the principal figures in it, was himself traditionally a playwright and wrote the play *Medea*, now lost. Be that as it may, reading *Poetaster* with that war in mind encourages one to give unwarranted weight to the business of Captain Tucca and his page and to the identification of Crispinus and Demetrius with playwrights Marston and Dekker. These matters merely confirm the theme and action of the play; they do not establish them.

Actually very little of Jonson's *Poetaster* is concerned with stage poetry. The comprehensive action of the play is to establish the ethical ground and function of all true poetry, regardless of type or occasion. Three kinds of poetry come up for consideration: Virgil's epic poetry, the kind written in full awareness of every citizen's obligation to state and society and ultimately a kind to be written only by the most gifted of poets; Horace's satire, a kind within the range of less exalted talents but still correctly regular in form and moral in intent; and finally, Ovid's kind of poetry, which carries with it no obligation for the author except an obligation to his own muse. Roughly speaking, the last of these kinds corresponds to the kind of poetry Marlowe had written (it is significant that Jonson uses Marlowe's translation of Ovid's *Amores*, I.xv, when he has the stage Ovid declare his faith in poetry); the second, Horace's kind, to the kind Jonson frequently wrote when he was not working at plays. The best, or Virgilian kind, corresponds to the poetry Jonson hoped eventually to write, perhaps as an English laureate (the translations of Virgil's poetry in the play are all Jonson's). Jonson exalts Virgil, of course, and he vindicates Horace. He also gives Ovid and the followers of Ovid's muse their due as writers of verse, occasionally of superb verse, but he repudiates their ideal, which in his view is pernicious. The other writers in the play, with the exception of Propertius, are all simply poetasters, and these Jonson rejects absolutely. This, in brief, is the main business of the play.

Ovid's intolerable ideal is presented in the very first scene, when young Ovid, having been urged by the servant Luscus to put on a face of industry to please his father, takes time out to read over—for himself and for us—some lines he has just finished writing (actually from "Elegy 15"). They defy Envy and deny the poet's obligation to serve public causes, praise the Greek and Roman poets by name, and conclude with the following claim to immortality:

> The suffering plough-share, or the flint may weare:
> But heauenly *poesie* no death can feare.
> Kings shall giue place to it, and kingly showes,
> The bankes ore which gold-bearing *Tagus* flowes.
> Kneele hindes to trash: me let bright PHŒBUS swell,
> With cups full flowing from the MVSES well.
> Frost-fearing myrtle shall impale my head,
> And of sad louers Ile be often read.
> "Enuie, the liuing, not the dead, doth bite:
> "For after death all men receiue their right.
> Then, when this bodie fals in funerall fire,
> My name shall liue, and my best part aspire.
>
> (1.i.73–84)

Offhand, one would be inclined to take this sort of thing as conventional hyperbole and hardly something to be considered seriously. If we do consider it seriously, however, we find that Ovid has claimed for poetry precisely the kind of autonomy that caused Plato to reject poetry's claims to respectability, declaring it a lie, an illusion, and a misleader of youth.[14]

Jonson himself, as we have seen, had already confronted Plato's objections and in *Every Man in His Humor* had used one of the traditional rejoinders.[15] The substance of Lorenzo's speech in Act v (iii.315–331) seems to be that poetry can do whatever philosophy can do and, as Sidney had insisted in his *Apologie for Poetrie*, do it much better.[16] Surely there was nothing in Lorenzo's long speech that could have caused an ordinary Elizabethan humanist to turn a hair; but Jonson was not ordinary, and he was well on his way to abandoning even this line of argument, as his exclusion of the passage from the 1616 version of *Every Man in His Humor* suggests. The Jonson of the major comedies was to see poetry as an extension of the man and, moreover, require poetry to work humbly and diligently in the world, not fly off into some empyrean. Young Lorenzo in 1598 may have preferred a poetry "That hates to haue her dignitie prophand, / With any relish of an earthly thought"; but once turned into the Edward Knowell of Jonson's 1616 version, he forgets such nonsense. That sort of thing belongs to the Ovids of this world, and it is Jonson's Ovid who lives and falls by it as a principle. At the end of the second scene of *Poetaster*, after an unpleasant encounter with his father, Ovid continues:

> O sacred *poesie*, thou spirit of artes,
> The soule of science, and the queene of soule,
> What prophane violence, almost sacriledge,
> Hath here been offered thy diuinities!
>
> (1.ii.231–234)

The Playwright in the Play

Poetry is the only true knowledge, he declares:

> When, would men learne but to distinguish spirits,
> And set true difference twixt those jaded wits
> That runne a broken pase for common hire,
> And the high raptures of a happy *Muse*,
> Borne on the wings of her immortall thought,
> That kickes at earth with a disdainefull heele,
> And beats at heauen gates with her bright hooues;
> They would not then with such distorted faces,
> And desp'rate censures stab at *poesie*.
> They would admire bright knowledge, and their minds
> Should ne're descend on so vnworthy obiects,
> As gold, or titles. . . .
>
> (1.ii.240–251

The last three lines here are prompted by the remarks of his father, just departed, that poets cannot earn a respectable living. The sympathy of almost any audience may be expected to swing to Ovid's side at this point. Sentimental convention usually has it that even the rider of an unruly Pegasus is to be preferred to a worshipper of Mammon. The progress of the play quickly reveals that the dilemma is a false one.

Sympathy for Ovid diminishes in Act II as he proceeds there to play his role of autonomous poet in society. Though he himself is a young man of genius, he runs with a group of poetaster-courtiers who are scarcely better than the group of caterpillars who threatened to corrupt the court in *Cynthia's Revels*. Shortly after the act begins, they all arrive at the house of one Albius, a jeweler, whose wife Chloe makes pretension to breeding and has ambitions to shine in courtly society. Only one of the group, Propertius, seems capable of genuine feeling; but he grieves so excessively for his beloved Cynthia,

43

recently dead, that before the play is over, he has lapsed into melancholy and shut himself up in her tomb (IV.iii.4–6). Ovid, himself a man of genuine feeling, understands Propertius' distress and sympathizes. "Worthy Roman!" he says. "Me thinkes I taste his miserie, and could / Sit downe, and chide at his malignant starres" (II.ii.57–59). And Ovid's own beloved, Julia, adds, "Me thinkes I loue him, that he loues so truly." Love itself, of course, is not discredited here; nor is there anywhere a suggestion that the affection of Ovid and Julia for one another—or, for that matter, of Propertius for the departed Cynthia—is insincerely professed or less than deep. The flaw in Propertius' love is that it is anarchic: it rests on no general sense of decorum and destructively becomes a law unto itself. This is the flaw in Ovid's devotion to poetry, as we have seen; and it is also the flaw in Ovid's love for Julia. For Julia is none other than daughter to the Emperor Augustus; and Ovid's attachment to her is reprehensible, certainly by Elizabethan standards if not by our own.

Even before the end of Act I Ovid had declared his love for Julia in suspiciously extravagant terms:

> IVLIA, the gemme, and iewell of my soule,
> That takes her honours from the golden skie,
> As beautie doth all lustre, from her eye.
> The ayre respires the pure *elyzian* sweets,
> In which she breathes: and from her lookes descend
> The glories of the summer. Heauen she is,
> Prays'd in her selfe aboue all praise: and he,
> Which heares her speake, would sweare the tune-full orbes
> Turn'd in his *zenith* onely.
>
> (I.iii.38–46)

When his friend Tibullus protests, "PVBLIVS, thou'lt lose thy selfe," Ovid replies with a concluding couplet: "O, in no labyrinth, can I safelier erre, / Then when I lose my selfe in praysing her" (1.iii.47–48). As courtly gesture this sort of thing is perhaps tolerable, particularly when applied to a Cynthia or an Elizabeth whose position makes it possible for the gesture to be an oath of allegiance: but Ovid is not swearing allegiance to the Emperor through his daughter. He is praising the Emperor's daughter as his mistress, in wild disregard for her safety and his own and for those proprieties on which the Roman state bases its hopes of survival. One must admit that Julia throughout Act II and in Act IV, where the two appear again in company with their sycophantic friends, behaves no more responsibly; but she is a woman and therefore, in Jonson's eyes, less responsible to begin with. She does, however, manage to deliver one telling remark. Act II concludes with a singing contest between Crispinus, the poetaster for whom the play is named, and Hermogenes, who is both poet and musician. Crispinus, a novice at singing, is actually rather modest; but Hermogenes, once persuaded to begin, cannot be persuaded to stop. As he threatens to sing yet another song, Julia observes, " 'Tis the common disease of all your musicians, that they know no meane, to be intreated, either to begin, or end" (II.ii.201–202). Her criticism neatly caps the whole scene; for nothing said or done here submits to rule, measure, or moderation. Ovid, for all his genius, is helpless in the company of poetasters that surrounds him.

By contrast Horace in Act III is easily able to keep his integrity, if not his person, out of the reach of Crispinus' anarchic grasp. Crispinus, now sure of his status as a poet, has asked for an introduction to Maecenas:

If thou would'st bring me knowne to Mecœnas, I should second thy desert well; thou should'st find a good sure assistant of mee: one, that would speake all good of thee in thy absence, and be content with the next place, not enuying thy reputation with thy patron. Let me not liue, but I thinke thou and I (in a small time) should lift them all out of fauour, both VIRGIL, VARIUS, and the best of them; and enioy him wholy to our selues. (III.i.238–246)

Horace answers him contemptuously with a denial and a principle:

> Sir, your silkenesse
> Cleerely mistakes MECŒNAS, and his house;
> To thinke, there breathes a spirit beneath his roofe,
> Subiect vnto those poore affections
> Of vnder-mining enuie, and detraction,
> Moodes, onely proper to base groueling minds:
> That place is not in *Rome*, I dare affirme,
> More pure, or free, from such low common euils.
> There's no man greeu'd, that this is thought more rich,
> Or this more learned; each man hath his place,
> And to his merit, his reward of grace:
> Which with a mutuall love they all embrace.
>
> (III.i.247–259)

Crispinus says he finds all this hard to believe, and Horace replies, "I am no torturer, to enforce you to beleeue it, but 'tis so." Lest readers in spite of all this somehow miss the principle that greatness of mind means knowing oneself and one's place, Jonson included it in his free adaptation of Horace's *Satire* 1, Book II, which he fashioned into a new scene for the Folio version of Act III. There the satirist Horace chafes under the rebukes of those who have accused him of following a pedestrian muse, "that thinke what euer I haue writ / Wants pith, and matter to eternise it" (III.v.3–4). The aged and wise jurist Trebatius urges him to try writing about

Caesar. "I feele defects in every facultie," Horace complains; "Great CAESARS warres cannot be fought with words." Trebatius suggests that he try writing about Caesar's peacetime virtues, and Horace modestly replies:

> Of that, my powers shall suffer no neglect,
> When such sleight labours may aspire respect:
> But, if I watch not a most chosen time,
> The humble wordes of FLACCVS cannot clime
> Th' attentiue eare of CAESAR; nor must I
> With lesse obseruance shunne grosse flatterie:
> For he, reposed safe in his owne merit,
> Spurnes backe the gloses of a fawning spirit.
>
> (III.v.29–36)

In the course of the satire, or scene, he comes to the realization that being true to his own nature is the important thing; and thus enlightened, he declares with confidence, "I will write *satyres* still, in spite of feare" (III.v.100).

With or without the Folio's added scene, the conflict in *Poetaster* has emerged by the end of Act III and may be described as the conflict between Ovid's glittering but amoral poetry conceived and written in anarchy and Horace's humble and morally sensitive satire.[17] In Act IV Ovid's licentious companions make their figurative assault upon heaven. They stage in Princess Julia's apartment at the Imperial Palace a banquet at which everyone assumes the part of some god or goddess. Tibullus, delivering the invitation to the jeweller's wife and the young lady staying at her house, explains:

> To tell you the femall truth (which is the simple truth) ladies; and to shew that *poets* (in spight of the world) are able to *deifie* themselues: At this banquet, to which you are inuited, wee intend to assume the figures of the Gods; and to giue our

> seuerall Loues the formes of Goddesses. Ovid will be Ivpiter;
> the Princesse Ivlia, Ivno: Gallvs here Apollo; you Cytheris,
> Pallas; I will bee Bacchus; and my Loue Plavtia, Ceres:
> And to install you, and your husband, faire Chloe, in honours,
> equall with ours; you shall be a Goddesse, and your husband a
> God. (iv.ii.37–47)

This is spoken half in jest and half in earnest; for the poets
acknowledge neither gods nor any other kind of authority
higher than themselves. Moreover, from being libertines in
poetry they propose to go further and be libertines in morals
also. Thus the only new status that remains to them is treason,
and it is a charge of treason that the actor from whom they
have sought to rent properties for their revels brings to the
sycophant Asinius Lupus and that Lupus brings to responsible authorities.

Unfortunately when Augustus Caesar, Maecenas, and Horace interrupt the courtiers' banquet, words that smack of
treason are indeed in the air, and Ovid is uttering them:

> Mercury, our Herald; Goe from our selfe, the great God
> Ivpiter, to the great Emperour, Avgvstvs Caesar: And com-
> mand him, from vs (of whose bountie he hath receiued his
> sir-name Avgvstvs) that for a thanke-offring to our benefi-
> cence, he presently sacrifice as a dish to this banquet, his
> beautifull and wanton daughter Ivlia. Shee's a curst queane,
> tell him; and plaies the scold behind his backe: Therefore, let
> her be sacrific'd. Command him this, Mercury, in our high
> name of Ivpiter Altitonans. (iv.v.200–210)

Julia is at the moment playing a wrathful Juno to Ovid's
lustful Jupiter, and she too manages to make a self-incrimi-
nating speech before she sees her father and falls terrified to

her knees. Penitence is vain at this point, however; Caesar commits her to prison, banishes her lover, and contemptuously rebukes the reveling libertine poets and poetasters:

> Are you, that first the *deities* inspir'd
> With skill of their high natures, and their powers,
> The first abusers of the vse-full light;
> Prophaning thus their dignities, in their formes:
> And making them like you, but counterfeits?
> O, who shall follow vertue, and embrace her,
> When her false bosome is found nought but aire?
> And yet, of those embraces, *centaures* spring,
> That warre with humane peace, and poyson men.
> Who shall with greater comforts, comprehend
> Her vnseene being, and her excellence;
> When you, that teach, and should eternize her,
> Liue, as shee were no law vnto your liues:
> Nor liu'd her selfe, but with your idle breaths?
>
> (iv.vi.34–37)

Thus does Caesar—and presumably Jonson—condemn a poetry, or any form of art, that proceeds on the assumption that it is its own excuse for being.

It should be noted, however, that Jonson does not entirely condemn Ovid the man or discredit his love for Princess Julia or even suggest that the young man's "treasonous" remarks were really treasonous. "Was this the treason? this, the dangerous plot, / Thy clamorous tongue so bellow'd through the court?" Horace asks of the sycophant Lupus (iv.vii. 37–38) as soon as Caesar has left the scene; and he proceeds to characterize the merrymaking as "innocent mirth" and "harmlesse pleasures, bred of noble wit." Moreover, in the leave-taking scenes which conclude the fourth act Ovid is clearly heartbroken, as is Julia, at the circumstances which now must separate them forever. The point to be made here is not that Ovid followed a will-o'-the-wisp instead of a muse or that he expended his energies in pursuit of a false love. The muse was good enough, but it was followed in the wrong way, in arrogance rather than in humility; it was a service greater than the god. So was the love a good thing, insofar as it was merely love of man for woman. The pity of it all—and it is pity only that we are supposed to feel here—was that the love of woman, like the love of poetry, was pursued as an absolute in utter forgetfulness of the superior love that citizens owe to their sovereign, whether they happen to be satirists or poets of love or lovers indeed. To make such an error is to commit the fatal breach of decorum and initiate the corruption of art and morals alike. To write bad poetry is reprehensible but forgivable. To worship any poetry for its own sake, whether good poetry or bad, is a sin and the prelude to disaster.[18]

Thus we are brought close to Jonson's dictum, soon to be articulated in the Epistle Dedicatory to *Volpone*, regarding "the impossibility of any mans being the good Poet, without first being a good man." This principle is fairly well stated in the banquet scene of *Poetaster*, where Caesar in his final words declines to forgive those who

> . . . liue in worship of that idoll, vice,
> As if there were no vertue, but in shade
> Of strong imagination, meerely enforc't?
> This shewes, their knowledge is meere ignorance;
> Their farre-fetcht dignitie of soule, a phansy;
> And all their square pretext of grauitie
> A meere vaine glorie: hence, away with 'hem.
> I will preferre for knowledge, none, but such
> As rule their liues by it, and can becalme
> All sea of humour, with the marble *trident*

Of their strong spirits: Others fight below
With gnats, and shaddowes, others nothing know.

(iv.vi.67–78)

Some might object that such a principle requires all who sub-
scribe to it to equate ethics with poetry and to make the poet
the first measure of his poem. Jonson, one imagines, would
have seen nothing at all wrong in doing either of these things.
Apparently he tried seriously in his maturity to do both; and
Poetaster, one of the last pieces of his artistic adolescence, may
be read as a deliberate attempt to map out and present concretely the philosophical terrain upon which the later and
greater comedies were to be erected. Nowhere was Jonson to
suggest, as he may have seemed to some to suggest in *Every
Man in His Humor*, that a poet might be the mindless vehicle
of some divine afflatus. Jonson always required his poet to
have native skill, respect for values discovered and established
by literary artists of the past, much reading, and much capacity for hard work.[19] If, in this last of his comical satires, he
had not yet gone so far as to declare the satirist ready for the
literary pantheon, he had at least laid the ground for such a
declaration. In the scene that he added to the Folio he did
declare that satirists—like wolves and bulls, he said (and, one
could legitimately add, like poets in general)—are born, not
made. He comes close to saying that a natively endowed
satirist should be credited with genius whenever he applies
his talent to the writing of a satire properly sanctioned and
aimed at men's crimes and not their persons. At any rate, such
is the implication of Act v of *Poetaster*, where the vindication
of an authorized satirist is the prime concern.

The last act of *Poetaster* is notorious for its purgation scene,
in which the poetaster takes Horace's pills and is relieved of
the crudities with which he has stuffed his offensive poem.

51

Much more attention, however, is given to establishing Horace's position with respect to Caesar and the supreme poet Virgil. In the first scene Caesar, Maecenas, Gallus, Tibullus, and Horace are all waiting to pay tribute to Virgil, who is to give a public reading from the *Aeneid*. Caesar asks the three poets to express freely their opinion of Virgil and suggests that Horace speak first as being "the poorest, / And likeliest to enuy, or to detract" (v.i.77–78). Horace immediately ingratiates himself with the spirited Emperor by respectfully but indignantly rejecting the notion that a poor man is always prone to envy:

> . . . knowledge is the *nectar*, that keepes sweet
> A perfect soule, euen in this graue of sinne;
> And for my soule, it is as free as CAESARS:
> For, what I know is due, I'le giue to all.
>
> (v.i.88–91)

He keeps his word and begins by praising the "rectified spirit" which is the fount of all that poet's "many reuolutions of discourse" and praises that discourse as being

> . . . so ramm'd with life,
> That it shall gather strength of life, with being,
> And liue hereafter, more admir'd, then now.
>
> (v.i.136–138)

The others agree; and Caesar, pleased, declares that their judgment "Argues a trueth of merit in you all."

The eminence of Virgil was established fact among Jonson's contemporaries also, of course; and Horace's reaffirmation of it in the play serves mainly to present Jonson's own analysis of the basis for greatness in a poet and by extension to suggest

Jonson's own magnanimity and lack of envy. Scene ii goes farther and provides a demonstration of the demeanor that is mandatory for even the greatest of poets whenever he happens to stand in the presence of his sovereign. In that scene Virgil, in spite of unanimous testimonials to his greatness and in spite of the self-knowledge that true genius confers, modestly declines to sit in the laureate's chair and read his verse until Caesar has expressly commanded him to do so. At Caesar's bidding, however, Virgil readily complies; and he is reading from the fourth book of his masterpiece when the play's almost forgotten fools rush in—sycophant Lupus and his minions, blustering Captain Tucca, poetaster Crispinus, and the weak-minded writer of plays Demetrius Fannius.

The purpose of their intrusion is to discredit Horace, but in this they fail and instead almost immediately begin to incriminate themselves. Caesar himself takes care of Lupus and his party. Then he orders Virgil to preside over a temporary tribunal set up to judge the other would-be detractors, particularly Crispinus and Demetrius. As every reader of Jonson's play will recall, Crispinus is made to take pills, administered by Horace, and purge himself of his fantastic vocabulary; both are forbidden ever to engage in detraction again whether at the booksellers', in taverns, in two-penny rooms, at tiring houses, or in noblemen's butteries. To Virgil's stern "Demand, what cause they had to maligne HORACE," the penitent Demetrius replies: "In troth, no great cause, not I; I must confesse: but that hee kept better company (for the most part) then I: and that better men lou'd him, then lou'd me: and that his writings thriu'd better then mine, and were better lik't, and grac't: nothing else" (v.iii.449–453). Thus in spite of the title and in spite of the postulated eminence of Virgil at the end, Horace is still the subject of this play and at the center of our interest in it. It concludes with the honest satirist completely vindicated and Caesar declaring to all assembled that

> It is the bane, and torment of our eares,
> To heare the discords of those iangling rimers . . .
> Let them fall,
> With their flat groueling soules: Be you your selues.
> And as with our best fauours you stand crown'd:
> So let your mutuall loues be still renown'd.
>
> (v.iii.615–616, 620–623)

All this can be, and apparently was, read as Jonson's vindication of himself as a man, as a poet, and as a satirist. We are free to judge as we like. Surely the principle is sound: given a solid terrain of impeccable ethics and the genius of perception and expression that poets have, we can occasionally get something to make us exclaim with Virgil, "The honest *Satyre* hath the happiest soule." This certainly applies to the historical Horace whom we all know, and it applies to the Horace in Jonson's play who maintained his sunny disposition even while giving vicious detractors the rebuke they deserved. It also seems applicable to Jonson. Moreover, the informed reader, mindful that two years after *Poetaster* a Stuart Caesar would replace England's Cynthia on the throne, aware that Jonson in presenting Virgil put forth his own version of Virgil's poetry (as opposed to Marlowe's version of Ovid), and aware of Jonson's hope of writing England's epic poem— a hope that vanished in flames with his unfortunate library and uncompleted manuscripts—such a reader may see in this play a barely suppressed hope as well as a vindication. Jonson continued to "correct" society even in his masterpieces; he never ceased to be England's satirist. But the dream that he might someday also "celebrate" in a form that would, like Virgil's poem, "live hereafter, more admired than now" must have especially brightened his horizon in 1601 as he temporarily abandoned comedy and proceeded to construct his first tragedy, *Sejanus*, and to plan others on Catiline and the English Mortimer.

CHAPTER THREE

Volpone

"Salt" for the Creative Talent

onson's announcement of his plan to turn to tragedy appeared, as we have seen, in the "Apologetical Dialogue" which was used in a single stage performance of *Poetaster* and thereafter suppressed until 1616, when it appeared in the Folio. In view of the unhappy fate of his tragedy *Sejanus* (1603), three lines in that announcement now seem almost prophetic: "... if I proue the pleasure but of one, / So he iudicious be; He shall b'alone / A Theatre vnto me ..." (ll. 226–228). As it turned out, more than one judicious patron approved the play; but the general audience at the Globe damned *Sejanus* at its first production, and Jonson for three more years turned out no plays at all that were solely his own. During this interval the writing of court masques and entertainments, for which the new queen, Queen Anne, had a predilection, absorbed some of his energy. He also collaborated with his friend George Chapman and a former enemy, John Marston, in the successful *Eastward Ho!;* but that play had lines in it that offended delicate Scottish sensibilities, and Jonson and his associates found themselves temporarily in prison as a result. The fact that Jonson was a recusant during this troubled period also added to his vexations and distractions.

All in all, Jonson's temporary holiday from comedy must have been only occasionally gratifying to him. He had set out on a new adventure with high hopes of escaping from the petty annoyances that dogged most popular playwrights; and the concluding lines of the "Apologetical Dialogue" to *Poetaster* indicate that, like his successor Milton, he thought himself justified in looking for a "fit audience though few":

> There's something come into my thought,
> That must, and shall be sung, high, and aloofe,
> Safe from the wolues black iaw, and the dull asses hoofe.
>
> (ll. 237–239)

After the failure of *Sejanus*, however, and the momentarily sobering consequences of his involvement in a collaboration, he returned to familiar territory and composed a new play of his own, *Volpone, or The Fox*—"fully penned," according to his Prologue, in five weeks.

Apparently *Volpone* was immediately successful. It was performed in London early in 1606 and later in that same year at the two universities, to whom Jonson dedicated "both it and himself" when he allowed the play to be printed in 1608.[1] As in all his previous comedies with the exception of *Every Man out of His Humor* and *Eastward Ho!* Jonson declined to use an English setting in *Volpone*, but this time he so completely particularized his scene that no would-be detractor could take it for anything but what it was declared to be, a play about Venice.[2] This time, moreover, he was writing that first example of what Kernan has called Jonson's Menippean satire, a broadly satirical kind of comedy that manages to do without the conspicuous satiric figure; henceforth to say his piece as author, Jonson would step outside the play, into a proper prologue or some other device, and characters like Asper, Crites, and Horace would not return to the dramatis personae.[3] (Clearly Jonson wanted people to laugh at *Volpone* rather than take it as an occasion for pointing fingers of scorn.[4] "All gall, and coppresse, from his inke, he drayneth," he wrote in his prologue; "Onely, a little salt remayneth." Unfortunately many readers have not been able to take this statement at face value. There are some who consider *Volpone* Jonson's darkest play, and some have even called it a tragedy.[5]

Volpone is not a tragedy, of course, but the heavy tone of it does create problems. Part of the somberness is due to what happens in the main series of episodes and part to what does not happen there. In the subplot we see two egregious fools rebuked and sent packing, as in comedies from time immemorial; but in the main plot we also see two victimizing scoundrels and three of their victims exposed, condemned, and sent to punishment. The subplot shows us a young man enjoying the taste of a petty revenge successfully but mistakenly pursued; and the main plot lets us see a colorless young woman released from a bad marriage and returned to her home, while her young defender, at first dispossessed by his father, is allowed to inherit during his father's lifetime. These rewards, however, are given and received without joy, and the punishments are severe by any standards. Furthermore, everything in *Volpone* comes about much as it does in some tragedies, and particularly as it does in Jonson's own *Sejanus* of three years before, in which a series of villains prey upon one another, as Albany says of humanity in *King Lear* (IV.ii.49–50), like monsters in the deep. Yet even in *Sejanus* Jonson has given us at the end a few sturdy Romans who become conspicuously wiser for their experience, and their presence on the scene encourages the hope of a season of civic health whenever the purgation of evil by evil shall be complete.[6] (There are no characters in *Volpone* who give us that kind of hope, and the corners of the human spirit which Jonson exposed by means of his principal figures in that play give us little cause for hope of any kind.) The result is a comedy which can be made to appear funny in the hands of a good producer but which is quite capable of giving ordinary audiences nightmares if they carry a memory of the performance home for serious reflection. For those attuned to Jonson's reverence for poetry, creativity, and the human capacity for invention, the effect of *Volpone* can be devastating indeed; for here human genius, given the reins, ends not in triumph but in perversion and corruption. Before judging the play absolutely, however, we shall do well to look at a few of its lighter aspects. It does have a few of these, though modern productions sometimes leave them out; and in them we find not only leavening for the work as a whole but a device for applying and evaluating the import of the darker parts. We shall also find there a faint suggestion of that self-important critic from comical satire whom Jonson apparently had not abandoned entirely but transformed, merged with a still older character type, and directed to uses other than that of speaking the author's mind.

Most of the lighter moments in *Volpone* occur in the subplot, or in those moments when subplot and main plot converge. In that part of the play we see two pretentious English travelers, a knight and his lady, talk themselves into incriminating situations, get exposed for the silly fools we have immediately perceived them to be, and thereafter hastily make their departure. Admittedly most of this business, both to see and to read, is less effective than the rest of the play; hence the aspects of *Volpone* that one usually remembers and talks about are those of the main plot, which deals with Volpone and his three Venetian victims. There we find the famous beast-fable story, which Robert Knoll has now identified as the legend of "The Fox Who Feigned Death";[7] that "double action" which unnecessarily disturbed John Dryden's sense of neatness;[8] and the theme of avarice which many, including Knoll, have taken to be the principal one in the play.[9] Even if our knowledge of *Volpone* is derived solely from some reduced acting version like the widely used one prepared several years ago by Stefan Zweig,[10] we can still read with profit much of the best criticism of the play—for example, Edward Partridge's brilliant discussion of Volpone's gold-centered world and a number of the shorter pieces alluded to in the notes to this chapter.[11] One of the few significant pieces of modern criticism that would be inconvenienced seriously by the permanent adoption of a *Volpone* bereft of its subplot would be an article by Jonas A. Barish, which, though conceding the "neatness" of modern versions, demonstrates convincingly the superiority of the complex whole as Jonson conceived and wrote it.[12] Barish's main point is that the subplot underscores and illuminates the main plot, principally with respect to three distinctive qualities that the figures in both plots exhibit—monstrosity, folly, and mimicry. This is certainly true enough; and were it not true, *Volpone* would be a very different kind of play. As Jonson wrote it, however, the play demonstrates in its main plot the frightening aspect of folly as it turns into crime while in the subplot it tends to sweeten the total effect with a healthy infusion of absurdities. Thus the story of the foolish Englishman and his wife leavens the story of the fox caught in his own trap and gives us a welcome opportunity to laugh now and then without feeling guilty. It also does considerably more than that.

Jonson has used his subplot, as Barish has also observed, to suggest parallels with England. He makes a reference there to a famous English tavern fool, the clown Stone, and to several "monstrosities," or natural phenomena, that had been well publicized in England shortly before the time of the play. All these Barish characterizes as "distant echoes of the moral earthquake rocking Venice."[13] One must demur at this point. Undoubtedly some of Jonson's more superstitious contemporaries, including perhaps a Sir Politic Would-Be or two in the audience, saw natural fools and wonders in just this light, but there is good reason to suspect that Jonson put them into this play more for contrast than for comparison. We note that two characters in the subplot talk about such things. One is that prodigy-minded knight, Sir Politic Would-Be, who knows of the raven's nesting in a naval vessel, of the lioness's whelping in the Tower, of Kepler's new star (who in Europe could have avoided knowing about that?), and of the strange fires at Berwick; he also recalls that porpoises have recently been seen in the Thames above London bridge. The other character is a sane and sophisticated young tourist, named Peregrine, who has been away from England only seven weeks. Peregrine's name means "traveler," of course; but Barish reminds us that it is also the name of a kind of hawk and that the hawk elsewhere in Jonson is described as a bird who "pursues the truth, strikes at ignorance, and makes the fool its quarry."[14] This, one recalls, is an apt description of the function of Downright in *Every Man in His Humor;* and Peregrine, within the much more limited scope allowed to moral indignation in this play, resembles closely the Downright, or Giovanni, from Jonson's earlier work. In this role of hawk he also resembles those more militant castigators of the comical satires; but as was noted earlier, he does not come to us in any sense a social reformer, he does not assume that role in the course of the action, and he does not speak in any special way for Ben Jonson. It is simply Peregrine, pursuer of truth, who reports the death of Master Stone and does so with an expression of regret in passing, "they doe lacke a tauerne-foole extremely" (II.i.54). Clearly there is nothing in this bare datum that invites us to equate the inspired clowning that can make a Stone famous with the degenerate and despicable kind of folly, however laughable, that characterizes Volpone's scavenging victims. Similarly, in the interest of truth, Peregrine is able to report a second whelping in the Tower, to give the precise number of porpoises that have been seen (six and a sturgeon also), and to add that a whale has been sighted as well; but it is obvious that he does not think of these natural wonders as being in any way akin to such physically monstrous creatures as inhabit Volpone's household. Nor does Peregrine share Sir Politic's belief that ravens, lion cubs, porpoises, and heavenly phenomena are signs and portents or that the whale in the Thames is a part of some Spanish plot. "This fellow / Do's he gull me, trow? or is gull'd," he gasps in astonishment as Sir Politic begins his questioning II.i.23–24). England has fools and monsters of its own, for Sir Politic and his lady have both come from there; but Jonson's focus in this play is not on the geographical extension of folly but upon the even wider theme that corruption, wherever it may be, breeds more corruption. The Would-Bes come to Venice as fools; they are lucky in the end to be able to leave as nothing worse. Peregrine at one point expresses surprise that a respectable woman like Lady Would-Be should take pleasure in such degenerate surroundings, and Sir Politic replies with a hoary cliché, "Yes, sir, the spider, and the bee, oft-times, / Suck from one flowre" (II.i.30–31). He is deceiving no one but himself; those who feed here are, for the moment at least, spiders all, and they feed from one poisonous blossom.

Thus the subplot lightens the rest of the play not merely by showing us venial folly as opposed to mortal, but by suggesting that elsewhere in societies equally human, there are wonders that we need not fear as prodigious monsters and innocent folly that can be enjoyed. Peregrine by his apparent good sense and his matter-of-fact reporting of such everyday things encourages us for a moment to ignore that suspension of judgment that we tend to make whenever we are confronted by something that presumably comes to us with the label of farce on it. In other words Peregrine's entrance constitutes a declaration that this exhibition is not farcical but relevant—at least a Menippean satire if not a Juvenalian one. In that way his presence, which usually marks the lighter moments in the play, tends briefly to make the gloom of the main action in *Volpone* seem darker than it might otherwise. At the same time, however, it also reminds us that neither Venice nor any other society is ever corrupt of necessity. This is consistent with Jonson's portrayals of the world in his other plays: nothing is ever absolutely incorrigible in the Jonsonian scene, and everyone is free to be better if he will.[15] Beyond the bound of that drawing-room and boudoir society which the Venetians inhabit is another world, we are assured, with people in it who try to live by a viable system of values that shows these Italians to be corrupt only as a consequence of their own bad choices; moreover the existence of that other society, which happens to be also the society of Jonson's audience, leaves alive the hope that ordinary humanity, marred only by normal hereditary imperfection, can achieve something like moral health. Fittingly Jonson brings Peregrine, his vehicle for optimism, on the stage at precisely that point where Volpone comes to the crisis in his action and plunges down the road that leads eventually to his defeat. This is the mountebank scene, to which we shall return for a closer ex-

63

amination after we have considered the general function of mimicry in *Volpone* and taken into account that attitude which *Volpone* as a whole implicitly recommends as being essential to health but which most of the characters in the play illustrate only by ignoring it altogether.

Mimicry, the third characteristic noted by Barish as linking the two parts of the play, performs two functions: it amuses, diverts, and enlightens from time to time; but more importantly it serves to keep before us one of the main themes of the play.[16] In the subplot mimicry appears near the end when Peregrine assumes a disguise and takes "revenge" on Sir Politic Would-Be (v.ii), but it virtually dominates the main plot; for mimicry is that activity by which Volpone differentiates himself from all the other monstrous fools who surround him. As a Brainworm with real genius, Volpone is the legitimate maker and satirist in this piece, the creator of masquerades that force men who come to them to show what they are and thus stand for judgment; and he succeeds admirably in his making until his continual failure to recognize and take into account his own human limitations sets him in the inevitable irreversible course to disaster.[17] For Volpone, in short, is a presumptuous poet like Ovid in *Poetaster* and goes the way of all proud fools who acknowledge no master and attempt to make their activity an end in itself[18] Almost all the other masquerading characters in the play have little or no control over the roles they assume; they are, as we spectators see clearly enough, really what their mask-names suggest they are, rapacious birds rather than human beings and move about in perpetual self-deception. This is true of Voltore, Corbaccio, and Corvino; but it is also true of Lady Would-Be, who acts out the role of garrulous parrot

that the "Pol" of her spouse's name suggests.[19] Throughout
the play she works very hard to wear another kind of mask
and hide the fact that all her sophistication is only a sterile
imitativeness, but her effort is futile. Never for a moment
does Lady Would-Be convince anyone else in the play that
her gentility is genuine, that she is fashionable, learned, or
beautiful, or that she is anything but a tedious mimic. Of all
the characters that circle about Volpone only Mosca manages
anything approaching the fox's kind of mimicry. Mosca has
a touch of Volpone's gift; he is, and he knows that he is, the
parasite supreme and thus has the parasite's ability to "change
a visor, swifter, then a thought" (III.i.29). Yet Mosca overreaches when he attempts to play *clarissimo*, and his final
performance succeeds only for as long as Volpone is willing to
tolerate it. In the end his parasite's masquerade collapses before the challenge of one genuinely to the manner born.

Volpone, by nature *fox* as well as *clarissimo*, knows himself better than any of these, and he alone projects the special
meaning that mimicry has in this play. His superadded roles
of senile decadent and Venetian mountebank are convincing
in themselves as masquerades and also amusing devices for
exposing the world he takes such obvious delight in bilking.
His fault is not in his vitality or his creativity but in his attitude toward these gifts and toward the world from which and
on which he works. To recognize that he creates out of sterility (which, in fact, is what he presumes to do when he emu-
lates the usurer and makes gold multiply) or out of corruption (which is what he does when he blasphemously feigns
death and attracts the lovers of death to his bedside) is to
recognize that Volpone is another example of Jonson's poet
gone wrong—a perverted artist who can only be made worse
if he persists in a failure to recognize his human limitations.

In short the human maker may be mischievous and seek forgiveness; but if he persists in playing God, he must inevitably create the engine that will destroy him. This is Volpone's situation, and his fault is the ancient and universal one of pride. One thinks again of Jonson's comment in the epistle about the impossibility of any man's being the good poet without first being a good man. Had Volpone been even potentially that good man, one surmises (that is, had he conceived of at least the possibility of pride in himself), he might have discovered, like Jonson's much less well-endowed actor-poet Asper-Macilente, his need to bend a humble knee at the end. Yet Volpone lacked the grain of grace, that insight into his limitations which might have enabled him to bring forth honest fruit; and his poetic activity yielded only the predictable harvest of rocks and thorns. Blind and incapable of learning to see, he was doomed from the beginning to suffer eventual defeat with all his fools.

The lacking "grain of grace" can also be described as humility, love, or charity, but none of these things characterizes Volpone. He is contemptuous of the world that gives him life and sustenance, provides normal men and most abnormal ones with their physical pleasures, and makes possible the sexual delight he comes to covet and the greater kind of human love of which he never has any comprehension. Moreover he recognizes no superior until that bright but evanescent moment when, as we shall see, he first encounters Celia, and even then his wonder dissolves in an impulse to possess and consume. In fact Volpone does not even indulge in that worship of gold which he counts on in all the others to serve as the magnet drawing them to his trap. The opening speech of the play is often quoted to illustrate just the opposite:

"Salt" for the Creative Talent

Good morning to the day; and, next, my gold:
Open the shrine, that I may see my *saint*.
Haile the worlds soule, and mine. More glad then is
The teeming earth, to see the long'd-for sunne
Peepe through the hornes of the celestiall *ram*,
Am I, to view thy splendor, darkening his:
That, lying here, amongs my other hoords,
Shew'st like a flame, by night; or like the day
Strooke out of *chaos*, when all darkenesse fled
Vnto the center.

(I.i.1–10)

This speech, which goes on for seventeen more lines and concludes—"Who can get thee, / He shall be noble, valiant, honest, wise"—is not a projection of Volpone's attitude but an
imaginative re-creation of attitudes that we are soon to find
well established in other characters in the play. Some have
said that the lines are a blasphemous parody of Christian
prayer, as indeed they are;[20] but this kind of blasphemy has
no roots in Volpone's own set of values. For him the only god
in sight is himself. This becomes clear as the scene advances.
Mosca, the parasite, who throughout the play will be ma-
neuvering secretly to snatch the role of miser for himself,
interrupts to say, "Riches are in fortune / A greater good
then wisedome is in nature." And to this Volpone replies
revealingly:

True, my beloued MOSCA. Yet, I glory
More in the cunning purchase of my wealth,
Then in the glad possession; since I gaine
No common way: I vse no trade, no venter;
I wound no earth with plow-shares; fat no beasts
To feede the shambles; haue no mills for yron,

Oyle, corne, or men, to grinde 'hem into pouder;
I blow no subtill glasse; expose no ships
To threatnings of the furrow-faced sea;
I turne no moneys, in the publike banke;
Nor vsure priuate—

(1.i.30–40)

Clearly Volpone would not really agree that riches are to be preferred to wisdom, if by the latter Mosca means the wisdom of the fox. To follow the metaphors of the play, one may say that while Voltore, Corvino, Corbaccio, and Mosca, like the scavenging creatures they are, love to anticipate consuming their golden bounty and perhaps hoarding it as well, Volpone, fox and hunter, worships nothing earthly save his own cleverness and rejoices mainly in the skill with which he catches and in the sport of devising new ways to catch. The others, corrupt and perverted as they are, love at least something; Volpone loves only himself. Even here at the beginning of the play he is fully embarked on his ingenious scheme of feigning a protracted death in order to attract legacy hunters; but it is the attracting that delights him, not the accumulation of treasure that the scavengers bring. Being free of temporal commitments—"no wife, no parent, child, allie" (which comprehensive statement, it should be noted, in effect disinherits Mosca)—Volpone is at liberty to create his own heir; and his "delay" in doing so brings daily new opportunities for foxlike creativity as people flock to his door:

Women, and men, of euery sexe, and age,
That bring me presents, send me plate, coyne, iewels,
With hope, that when I die, (which they expect
Each greedy minute) it shall then returne,
Ten-fold, vpon them. . . .

(1.i.77–81)

Secure in his apparent triumph over greedy humanity, he does not foresee the less happy occasion that will challenge his ingenuity. It does not occur to him that his own Mosca may soon seek to change roles and assume not only the status of heir from which the phrase "no allie" has just excluded him but the rank of *clarissimo* as well. When this does in fact happen, Volpone will have no choice but to "invent" a trick that will end all tricks and return the presumptuous Mosca to his parasite's role and a parasite's proper punishment. That he must lose his own freedom at this point seems less important to him than that he can triumph in principle and receive a punishment befitting a person of his superior rank, villainy, and wit. Volpone, in short, ends the play still the fox and still on top; but his self-centered world abides as the only world he knows or can ever know.

Preoccupation with self is really at the root of all the criminal or near-criminal folly in *Volpone*, and the play makes that evident in several ways, though the root itself is hidden below the surface for much of the time. On the glittering surface we find that punishments assigned reflect fairly well the severity of the faults they are supposed to be correcting. Mosca, of course, goes to the galleys for reason of status ("being a fellow of no birth, or bloud"); but the Hospital of the Incurables does seem an appropriate ending for Volpone, as do ridicule and torment on the pillory for the imaginary cuckold Corvino, repentance at San Spirito for old Corbaccio, and banishment for Voltore. We note with satisfaction that Sir Politic and his wife, whose sins consisted mainly in being vain and stupid, get off with simple embarrassment. Furthermore Jonson himself went out of his way in the Epistle Dedicatory to say that he had given considerable thought to the matter of punishment in *Volpone:*

And though my *catastrophe* may, in the strict rigour of
comick law, meet with censure, as turning back to my promise; I desire the learned, and charitable criticism to haue so
much faith in me, to thinke it was done off industrie: For,
with what ease I could haue varied it, neerer his scale (but
that I feare to boast my owne faculty) I could here insert. But
my speciall ayme being to put the snaffle in their mouths, that
crie out, we neuer punish vice in our *enterludes*, &c. I tooke
the more liberty; though not without some lines of example,
drawne euen in the ancients themselues, the goings out of
whose *comœdies* are not always ioyfull, but oft-times, the
bawdes, the seruants, the rituals, yea, and the masters are
mulcted: and fitly, it being the office of a *comick-Poet*, to
imitate iustice, and instruct to life, as well as puritie of language, or stirre vp gentle affections. (ll. 109–123)

According to some, what Jonson has produced herewith his
"industrie" is a sophisticated moral exemplum; and it is not
surprising that morally sensitive critics have expressed less
uneasiness about the ending of *Volpone* than they have about
the ending of Jonson's brighter comedies, where fairly serious
offenses are either ignored or pardoned.[21]

We get a better notion of the ethic at work in this play,
however, from the little entertainment that takes up the first
half of the second scene and gives us a burlesque of Pytha-
gorean metamorphosis as Jonson derived it from Lucian's
Gallus by way of Erasmus' translation. Ostensibly, at least,
this device points to Jonson's comic employment of the theme
of inheritance and adumbrates the rude awakening that is in
store for Volpone's victimized suitors in the fifth act of the
play,[22] but more importantly it says something about Volpone's "wisdome." "Fooles, they are the onely nation / Worth
mens enuy or admiration" goes the song at the end; and the
dénouement of the play as a whole lends credence to that

sentiment. The immediate point of the little song is that Androgyno, Volpone's household hermaphrodite, playing himself in the interlude, has just been declared the ultimate recipient of what was in the beginning a gift of purest intelligence straight from Apollo himself. Progressively degenerate in the descent, this Apollonian soul has manifested itself at one point in the famous philosopher Pythagoras, "that iuggler diuine," and then declined rapidly through a succession of permutations—prostitute, cynic, Carthusian monk, garrulous lawyer, braying mule, Puritan—until finally it has come to rest in the most unlikely figure of all, Androgyno, who is nothing positively, not even man or woman, but a fool; and there for want of anywhere else to go it remains.

Volpone says that he likes this "pretty invention," but he does not grasp much of the significance of it; and one of the implications that neither he nor Mosca, who wrote the interlude, senses at this point is that not even Apollonian wisdom, or creative wit, is enough to make up for the lack of a stable order which can give such wisdom its due place and meaning. In the anarchic world which these two have "created" for themselves and in which they elect to live, nothing can ever be certain. The creative wit, to which they both in turn lay claim, once given its independence can only degenerate and find rest in the one firm place left to it, at the bottom, in the body of a fool. This is the point of the concluding exchange between Androgyno and Nano the dwarf, who asks whether Androgyno's delight is due to his being able to vary his pleasure. Androgyno replies:

> Alas, those pleasures be stale, and forsaken;
> No, 'tis your Foole, wherewith I am so taken,
> The onely one creature, that I can call blessed:
> For all other formes I haue prou'd most distressed.
>
> (1.ii.55–58)

In all Volpone's world the hermaphrodite is the only one not fatally committed to self-satisfaction. Yet even in a world like this there are degrees, if only degrees of degeneracy. It is better to be a foolish gull than to be a guller. It is better—or perhaps only less undesirable—to be avaricious old Corbaccio, whose attempts to gull Volpone and his own son are as ludicrously feeble as they are futile, than it is to be Volpone, who gulls with skill and verve but fails utterly to see his fatal flaw in prideful boasting that he gains in no common way. Herein is at least some of the negative part of the instruction to life that Jonson provided in *Volpone*.

The positive part should involve a recognition of the moral order that informs the world, and it should tell us something of the rewards that may come to the virtuous people that inhabit there. Unfortunately the play does not delineate this aspect of things with much vigor, and that fact as much as anything else explains why *Volpone* has seemed more like tragedy than comedy to many of its admirers over the years. Still, as has already been suggested, the subplot of the play now and again points in the direction of positive values, and we get a hint of what such values may be if we listen carefully to Sir Politic's speech at the beginning of Act II:

> Sir, to a wise man, all the world's his soile.
> It is not *Italie*, nor *France*, nor *Europe*,
> That must bound me, if my fates call me forth.
> Yet, I protest, it is no salt desire
> Of seeing countries, shifting a religion,
> Nor any dis-affection to the state
> Where I was bred (and, vnto which I owe
> My dearest plots) hath brought me out; much lesse,
> That idle, antique, stale grey-headed proiect
> Of knowing mens minds, and manners, with VLYSSES:
> But, a peculiar humour of my wiues,

Laid for this height of *Venice,* to obserue,
To quote, to learne the language, and so forth—

(II.i.I–I3)

His companion Peregrine, whose name, whatever else it
means, suggests that he is accustomed to traveling, is clearly
interested in the world he sees unfolding before him and is
eager to learn from it. Sir Politic by contrast pretends to be
disdainful even of seeing. His serious fault (for folly pure and
simple could be excused and might even make him blessed)
lies in his rejection of that "idle, antique, stale, grey-headed
proiect" which makes the better part of the world kin; but he
is not the only one who has erred in this fashion. Near innocent that he is, Sir Politic has actually rejected the world with
less finality than almost anyone else in the play—except perhaps people like Bonario and Celia, about whose human attri-
butes and inclinations we know next to nothing. The principle
which this play assumes but almost keeps out of sight is that
the happy man will accept and respect the world and all that's
in it, love and let live, and not seek to possess, use, or abuse.
The reward for observing this principle is kinship, a bond of
love with other humane human beings, such as became visible in the bright performance of Justice Clement at the end
of *Every Man in His Humor.* But we see nothing of that bond
here, and without it all the characters in the play must remain
isolated. The sad thing about *Volpone* is that there is so little
love in it; the really frightening thing is that almost everybody in it is alone.

The loneliness of the principal characters in *Volpone* is
thrown into painful relief by the three mountebank scenes at
the beginning of Act II. These scenes, set as they are in the
open air and sunlight of St. Mark's Piazza before Corvino's

house, call to mind the Italy of casual roguery and habitual gaiety; and they contrast sharply with the other scenes in the play, most of which take place indoors, in an atmosphere suggestive of torchlight and heavy draperies and give us that morbid Venice symbolized by the carrion seekers. Here, as we have noted, stands Sir Politic delivering the speech about his disaffection for travel. Around him are all the sights that people have long made a point of coming to Venice to see, palaces, happy people, and pigeons; but he goes on blindly discoursing about the latest events in England and misinterpreting even these. The crowd in the Piazza pay little attention to him, however; for the famous Scoto of Mantua has just arrived and is about to put on his medicine show. That this Scoto is a charlatan and an imposter, and would be the first of these even if he were the real Scoto, is of no consequence on a sunny day in the Piazza. The point of his presence for the crowd of people who follow him is that he provides a colorful focus for a day that has no prescribed festival. He is the welcome occasion for a pleasant coming together that reaches its natural climax when the great lady at the window, Celia, with the traditional gesture of noblesse obliterates the distance between palace and yard and rewards their common entertainer. No one who understands Italy or the play or, for that matter, Jonson's England would imagine for a moment that Celia is deceived by Volpone's spiel or even that she takes it to be an example of great rhetoric. She is simply playing her part in the communal game.

Indeed, as Barish has pointed out, Volpone's spiel here breaks practically all the requirements of sophisticated rhetoric; and the point is a good one.[23] It is certainly not lost on Peregrine, who ranks Volpone's rhetoric with the vulgar rantings of the Puritan divine Broughton; but Sir Politic, who is far less sophisticated than Peregrine or Celia or the crowd of delighted Italians, takes the whole business as a serious effort at persuasive communication. Having just finished misinterpreting reports of the whelping lioness and honest porpoises above London bridge, he now gulps down a fraud that no one has really expected him to swallow, accepts for true report things that are patently fabrications, takes at face value Volpone's declarations of disinterestedness, and calls his language rare. Interestingly that "rare" language differs very little from the equally spurious rhetoric of his own wife, who a bit later in a determined attempt to impress Volpone will so mistake the effect of her own verbiage that she will come close to driving the magnifico out of his mind. "Troubled with noise, I cannot sleepe," Volpone will complain in that later scene; "I dreamt / That a strange *furie* entred, now, my house, / And, with the dreadfull tempest of her breath, / Did cleaue my roofe asunder (III.IV.40–43). But the parrot woman's tempest of words will continue with fragments of medicine, philosophy, literary criticism, and psychology until Volpone prayerfully beseeches, "Some power, some fate, some fortune rescue me" (III.IV.126).

The effect of Volpone's verbiage on Celia in the mountebank scenes is very different, but different for reasons that have nothing whatever to do with any efficacy in bringing people together. Volpone approaches Celia here precisely as any successful creative artist approaches his patron; and were he a proper maker, the effect of his approach—a public demonstration of gratitude—should be as satisfying to him as it obviously is to her. Volpone, however, has the talent of a Jonsonian poet but not that poet's fundamental goodness or his instincts. Succeeding in the presence of Lady Celia means to him only that he must press on and seek to possess her, consume her, like the fox he really is. Thus for Volpone the mountebank scenes become his moment of decision, the point at which he decides to forgo a true professional's triumph and instead launch his fatal assault upon Celia's chastity. "Shall I hope?" he asks Mosca soon after his return home; and Mosca's reply, wiser perhaps than he knows, is, "I will not bid you to despaire of aught, / Within a humane compasse" (II.iv.19–20).

Some would question the appropriateness of Mosca's response here and argue that Celia is not only not divine but scarcely alive.[24] Yet Jonson's naming of most of the other characters in *Volpone* seems to be precision itself, and we should allow to anyone named as she is at least the status of an unexamined ideal. She is certainly an unexamined ideal to Volpone, who never thinks to examine or "appreciate" any piece of treasure he collects; and she is also his unexamined and hence unrecognized opportunity. Up to this crucial moment his performances have not been entirely reprehensible. As a fabricator or poet Volpone has invariably, if unintentionally, presented honest poems. The masquerades in his boudoir have not been fundamentally false things. They have revealed accurately what most of the sophisticated Venetians in the play really are, morbid and moribund scavengers feeding on one another. Moreover, in his happier masquerade, performed before a happier part of Venice, he has simply made visible the capacity of a generous citizenry to indulge in games and make-believe. Celia is charmed by the latter performance, as are Peregrine and the crowd generally; and we are charmed, too, insofar as we have a capacity for enjoying the fantastic. We also recognize that all of Volpone's performances have been fantastic in much the same way and that as nets for the unwary they have served to catch only fools like Lady Politic and villains like Voltore, Corbaccio, and Corvino. In short, Volpone's masquerades are of the sort that would leave him unstained at the end and ready for forgiveness could he—like Brainworm in the earlier *Every Man in His Humor* and Jeremy-Face of *The Alchemist* shortly to come—take esthetic delight in his masquerading and then surrender it all at the end to some appropriate "magistrate," a Justice Clement or a Lovewit or even a Celia, and seek pardon for "the wit of his offence."[25] Thus at this point Volpone is not irremediably immoral. Before him stands his queen, with a name appropriate to the opportunity she presents; and he has only to see and sue for grace. It is the moment of testing, but Volpone neither sees nor understands.

In addition to the happier course open to him, Volpone has a choice of two courses leading to disaster. One of these he can follow simply by continuing his old practice of trying in each performance to surpass the former one, falsely confident that in his perpetual climbing he will never have to beware the consequences that came to Ovid in his folly and arrogance. The other he can follow by abandoning for the moment his pure delight in "gaining no common way" and prostituting his "poeticizing" to gain a nonesthetic end—in this case, the favors of Celia, Corvino's wife. For the moment he tries the second course, letting lust rather than avarice deflect him from his pleasure in exercising his much vaunted creative ingenuity; but before the play is over he will have resumed his furious participation in the first also. In any event by the end of Act III Volpone is already too far gone for redemption; by one path or another he is headed on an irreversible course to his mortification in the Hospital of the Incurables.

A brief comparison with Mosca may be useful at this point; for Mosca, though less bountifully endowed with creative spirit, learns at the middle of the play to imitate his master's action and heads on a parallel course of his own to destruction. It is at the beginning of Act III that he decides to step out from beneath the protective umbrella that his master has always provided and become autonomous:

> I Feare, I shall begin to grow in loue
> With my deare selfe, and my most prosp'rous parts,
> They doe so spring, and burgeon; I can feele
> A whimsey i' my bloud: (I know not how)
> Successe hath made me wanton. I could skip
> Our of my skin, now, like a subtill snake,
> I am so limber.
>
> (III.i.1-7)

At the end of this speech he is saying that to be a perfect parasite he must

> Present to any humour, all occasion;
> And change a visor, swifter, then a thought!
> This is the creature, had the art borne with him;
> Toiles not to learne it, but doth practise it
> Out of most excellent nature.
>
> (III.i.28-32)

Here, though claiming credit for creativity by nature, he is really declaring what he has learned from Volpone; but in any case he is now ready to make trial of his gifts and attempt an invention of his own. The proof of his subservience is that he begins at the very point to which Volpone has already descended. He will proceed immediately to prostitute his talents (though his occasion for doing so is an onset of avarice rather than of lust) and in the end ignore entirely the inventor's responsibility to offer the results of his activity to a patron. For this latter failure Mosca has no excuse whatever. At the beginning he created a poetic interlude and gave that unhesitatingly to his master. Volpone is still there and still his lord and, moreover, will ask specifically at the appropriate time for what is his due. Yet at that point Mosca, still touched with a parasite's ambition, will repudiate the chance for redemption that was available to Brainworm in the humor play; and Mosca's ending therefore can only be a despair similar to Volpone's and very like the despair that must have come to Asper-Macilente had it not been for the Queen's gracious condescension.

A mental review of Mosca's progress from folly to defeat should help us bring into focus the unity of a similar but more extensive pattern with Volpone at the center. It also should help us to see that the assault on Celia in Act iii is not simply the climax of one plot strand, as Dryden perhaps would have it, but the climactic point in the emergence of the main theme of the play. Here Volpone's series of devices begin to show for what they really are: steps toward that inevitable trapping of the fox in his own engine. In Act i he has shown how his capacity for creation can make him satyr-prince over all the avaricious fools in the world about him, including those who may be drawn to it from outside. To his poem of death they come like the carrion eaters they are. In Act ii he has created another poem, this time one in which he presents himself in the image of the giver and restorer of life; but his portrayal of Scoto of Mantua is actually a burlesque of the life-giver, capable of fooling no one except an ass like Sir Politic; and Celia, who seeks neither gold nor the fruits of lust, rewards it for what it is—a trivial poem but a poem nevertheless. In all this activity the bounty that has come to Volpone has been incidental to the delight he has gained from participating in it. Now in Act iii he deliberately seeks to take possession of something specific. He is no longer either the man who delights in gaining "no uncommon way" or an inspired mountebank to be sufficiently rewarded with the sight of a handkerchief fluttering from a beautiful hand at a window. He is a poet turned rhetorician, using words to persuade, and determined, if words fail, to win by any means at all. In short he is now tangled in his own net, and he has begun to be rapacious in the same sense as his scavenging victims. He has committed the unpardonable but inevitable sin for all patronless poets: he has corrupted creativity itself.

The setting for this is a room in Volpone's house. Young Bonario, son of old Corbaccio, having come to get proof of his father's willingness to disinherit him, has been hidden in a closet. Volpone is playing his "dying" role to perfection, as Mosca leads in Corvino, willing and eager to prostitute his wife, provided the gift will bring him to the height of Volpone's favor. In the conversation that takes place as Celia is led to Volpone's bed, the question of honor is posed, and Corvino declares that, Volpone being aged and infirm, no possible harm can come to the woman's honor or her person and certainly none to her reputation if no one outside is the wiser.[26] He is frank to admit, however, that he is asking her cooperation with a view to his own financial gain. Celia's despairing cry as he leaves her to face disgrace alone is as follows:

> O God, and his good angels! whether, whether,
> Is shame fled humane brests? that with such ease,
> Men dare put off your honours, and their owne?
> Is that, which euer was a cause of life,
> Now plac'd beneath the basest circumstance?
> And modestie an exile made, for money?
>
> (III.vii.133–138)

Two of Celia's questions here should be given special attention. She has asked whether men will corrupt the act of procreation in order to make money; and Volpone answers this one as he leaps from the couch, "I, in CORVINO, and such earth-fed mindes, / That neuer tasted the true heau'n of loue." He might also add, were he so minded, that he himself is not seeking to corrupt in this manner and that he has no interest in financial gain. Celia's first question, however, is whether it is possible that men can deliberately put off their honor and God's; and this is a question that applies directly to Volpone, who in diverting for his private pleasure what should have been a gift for some god, lord, or patron has committed an act far more shameful than Corvino's. In Celia's terms, he has put off God's honor, not simply his wife's or his son's or his own.[27]

Volpone's formal poem, his song to Celia, shows this unmistakably. It begins:

Come, my Celia, let us proue
While we can, the sports of loue,
Time will not be ours, for euer,
He, at length, our good will seuer;
Spend not then his gifts, in vaine.
Sunnes, that set, may rise againe:
But if, once, we lose this light,
'Tis with us perpetuall night.

(III.vii.165–172)

This is sheer blasphemy. Andrew Marvell's seduction poem, written a good many years later in the century, would have the grace to say:

But at my back I always hear
Time's winged chariot hurrying near:
And yonder all before us lie
Deserts of vast eternity.

("To His Coy Mistress," ll. 21–24)

81

There is a great difference between Jonson's "perpetual night" and Marvell's "deserts of vast eternity." The one makes of any activity here on earth—whether money-grubbing, sex, or poetry—an end in itself; for, as the lines indicate, there is nothing but nothingness beyond. The other does at least acknowledge an eternity and, moreover, an eternity with unexplored areas in it. Thus Volpone in his assault on Celia, or heaven as her name suggests, has not only turned poetry into rhetoric; he has denied God and by implication anyone else superior to his own needs. Immediately he adds to this cardinal blasphemy the inevitable proposal to make private use of all the gains that the others have been seeking to possess—pearls, diamonds, exotic foods, and even the phoenix itself, compounded of life and death, were that possible. And finally, seeing that neither rhetoric nor lust nor wealth can move one "whose innocence is all she can think wealthy, or worth th' enjoing," he resorts to naked unlovely force.

From this point on Volpone's inevitable failure as machinator is surely manifest to a perceptive reader or spectator. No moment for him was so happy as that instant when Celia's fluttering handkerchief signaled the success of his actor's poem, but the happiness of that moment was something he was incapable of perceiving. Now with no one at all to say, "Well done," and with no thought of seeking anyone to say it, he must return to his old practice of making poetry an end in itself. Mosca is there, but Mosca's applause has always been meaningless; for Mosca is neither lord nor gracious lady but only a parasite, a fly in deed as well as in name. This, of course, he proves openly to be at the last when Volpone, frantically seeking to recover his identity, asks Mosca to acknowledge that his master is alive. Mosca's refusal becomes the signal for the exposure and punishment of both, the prince of fools and his hopeful usurper. For Volpone, as has already been suggested, punishment befitting his rank and achievement is the only suggestion of a victory that can now come to him; but perhaps that much is preferable to obscurity.

One thing should be said in Volpone's favor: he does not, like Downright or Asper, presume to sit in judgment on the folly and villainy he takes so much delight in scourging. As we have also seen, he is continuously guilty of imagining that his art is self-sufficient and once of trying to make it serve his lust. That is, he stands in company with Ovid of *Poetaster* as one inclined either to exalt his art unduly or to use it improperly; and although capable of being vexed in the extreme, he shows no inclination to correct his victims or to save the rest of society from their kind. Such a function requires something like righteous indignation, and the only characters in the play who show any capability for that are the young people in it—Celia, Bonario, and Peregrine.

Of these only Peregrine, perhaps, has the energy to be the kind of crusading reformer that turned up in Jonson's early plays, first as Downright and then as satirist, and would appear again in the major plays following *Volpone*. All three of the young people make judgment on their fellow men in response to threats on their person; but while Celia and Bonario, like the ordinary citizens that they are, refer their case to the courts, Peregrine goes on to devise and execute punishment. The irony of this is that whereas Celia and Bonario have ample cause to take revenge, Peregrine really has none. What sets him off is Lady Would-Be's wildly improbable charge that he is a whore in male clothing. She retreats from that charge almost immediately, but so intense is Peregrine's pique that he translates her embarrassed attempt at mollification into the equally improbable fiction that she herself is a whore and her husband, a pimp. Peregrine has now become afflicted with a blindness more serious than that of Sir Politic, who is at least halfway aware that his fantasies are merely fantasies and under pressure can repudiate them. Thus all that Peregrine accomplishes in his "revenge" is the shaming of a relatively innocuous ninny who intended him no harm and in fact did him none. One may toy with the speculation that he will go on to develop the unlovely humor of other Jonsonian reformers, play Downright to those close to him and Macilente-Asper to society in general. Eventually, however, one hopes, he will also stumble upon the moral of Mosca's interlude and learn that it is sometimes better to be a fool and lose a contest than to be proudly victorious. Unfortunately there is no Cynthia in sight to save Peregrine from himself and bestow that moral as a gift of inspiration. He plays his part briefly and vanishes into obscurity with questions about his fate unanswered. Readers seem not to have cared greatly. Fortunately for Ben Jonson, the unseen Asper to Peregrine's Macilente, the sister universities stood ready, like twin Cynthias, to receive both his dramatic poem and the moral judgments implicit in it and thus relieve him of the infectious burden of pride in the one and pharisaical satisfaction in the other. Jonson was not again to be trapped in his own engine as he had been in the comical satires. He spoke his piece in an Epistle Dedicatory, but this time he himself was not judged by his own play.

The main plot of *Volpone* moves with mounting intensity through the last two acts toward the dénouement and the full revelation of its themes. The function of the long trial scene which occupies most of Act IV is to present Volpone in one more "good show" and to let that show begin to demonstrate, as the others have not demonstrated, the futility of such presumably self-sufficient triumphs. Neither Volpone nor his victims have any way now to terminate their activities. In one way or another he must continue to "die," and the other carnivores must continue to corrupt themselves. Thus in this scene Lady Would-Be kisses carrion, and Voltore makes a magnificent mockery of justice; even the other members of the judiciary become infected and seem uneasily eager to begin to taint themselves. Bonario, whose name calls goodness to mind, looks on with only an occasional weak comment; for it is not his function to punish or destroy, as he now knows only too well. Celia, who was ever willing to applaud Volpone the poet, can only shudder at the diabolical machinations that the poet perverted has proved capable of. She and Bonario perhaps already know what the first Avocatore will be able to pronounce only at the end of the play:

> Let all, that see these vices thus rewarded,
> Take heart, and loue to study 'hem. Mischiefes feed
> Like beasts, till they be fat, and then they bleed.
>   (v.xii.149–151)

Voltore, Corvino, Corbaccio, and Lady Would-Be are fat and bleeding already. Mosca, coolly controlling the situation for his own purposes, is still unscarred; but his time is shortly to begin. Volpone, whose creativity has been the means whereby their sins can be made known, stands ripe for the greatest punishment of all, the punishment that follows both human and angelic pride; and when it comes in Act v, it will be a punishment that he has devised for himself. The judge will say there at the end:

> And, since the most was gotten by imposture,
> By faining lame, gout, palsey, and such diseases,

Thou art to lie in prison, crampt with irons,
Till thou bee'st sicke, and lame indeed.

(v.xii.121–124)

This will be Volpone's bleeding and his fire. Like Dante's
damned he is destined to lie in a circle of his own choosing.

Our awareness of these matters begins to achieve fulness
in the remarkably revealing first two scenes of Act v, in which
Volpone appears once more at his house, having just returned
from his triumph at the Scrutineo. His pleasure in that triumph, however, is less than complete:

I ne're was in dislike with my disguise,
Till this fled moment; here, 'twas good, in priuate,
But, in your publike. . . .

(v.i.2–4)

Suddenly the fear strikes him that his acting perhaps was not
entirely acting:

'Fore god, my left legge 'gan to haue the crampe;
And I apprehended, straight, some power had strooke me
With a dead palsey: well, I must be merry,
And shake it off. A many of these feares
Would put me into some villanous disease,
Should they come thick vpon me: I'le preuent 'hem,
Giue me a boule of lustie wine, to fright
This humor from my heart.

(v.i.5–12)

Drinking momentarily restores him:

'Tis almost gone, already: I shall conquer
Any deuice, now, of rare, ingenious knauery,
That would possesse me with a violent laughter,

86

Would make me vp againe! So, so, so, so.
This heate is life; 'tis bloud, by this time.

(v.i.13-17)

The significance of this scene, or soliloquy, is that Volpone is
now beginning to face the consequences, not of poetry perverted to rhetorical uses (the sort of perversion he committed
when he tried to rape Celia and for which he has just escaped
punishment) but of poetry considered a self-sufficient thing,
an end in itself. He is confronting the despair of the patronless
poet, which is the same as that of the satirist without a sovereign; for in such a situation both poet and satirist are committed to an endless series of achievements, each surpassing
its predecessor, and each new achievement must prove finally
to be as unsatisfying as the one that went before. His fate is
like that of a person addicted to narcotics. The satisfactions of
gratification are evanescent, but the pangs of total withdrawal
are too terrible to contemplate.

The second scene of Act v gets Volpone moving again, and
it does so in a renewed context of the play's principal metaphors and themes. We have there almost an epitome of the
play: the worship of gold with which the whole business began, the metaphor of trade used throughout to link Volpone's
activity with the principal occupation of his native Venice,
the masquerade, the temptation theme, and the theme of
death. Volpone's new plan is as simple as it is inevitable: he
will reportedly return to that "death-bed" where he committed his temporary aberration and continue on what once
seemed to be a safe and highly successful course. This time,
however, he will pretend to be dead rather than dying and
leave the manipulation of victims to his executive officer Mosca, who will play the role of true heir and one by one disabuse
all the victims of their dream of inheriting.

87

Volpone miscalculates in assuming that Mosca, who does not share his master's weakness for sex, also does not share the weakness of Voltore, Corvino, and Corbaccio for yellow gold. Thus he is genuinely startled to learn that Mosca has never like himself rejoiced "more in the cunning purchase of . . . wealth, / Then in the glad possession." Mosca's miscalculation, however, is more serious; he fails to see that Volpone's pride in his cunning will not let him accept passively any serious challenge to that cunning. In fact, where cunning is at issue, Volpone must win the contest, even if winning means sacrificing both wealth and civic reputation. We in the audience wonder why these two do not listen here to some of their own observations. Volpone expresses amazement that Voltore, Corvino, and Corbaccio "should not sent [scent] some-what, or in me, or thee, / Or doubt their own side" (ll. 21–22). And Mosca replies, "True, they will not see't. / Too much light blinds 'hem, I thinke." Too much light blinds Mosca and Volpone as well, but neither of them notices. As Volpone is in the process of racing ahead with plans for his final coup, Mosca is openly declaring his fatal admiration for Volpone's gold:

> It transformes
> The most deformed, and restores 'hem louely,
> As 't were the strange poeticall girdle. Iove
> Could not inuent, t'himselfe, a shroud more subtile,
> To passe Acrisivs guardes. It is the thing
> Makes all the world her grace, her youth, her beauty.
>
> (v.ii.100–105)

Volpone still does not heed. He has been momentarily distracted by the delicious thought that Lady Would-Be, who has just made a show of kissing him in open court, may really be attracted to his person as well as to his wealth. He credits her readily with routine human avarice; yet pride will not let him suspect that anyone whom he might take into full confidence, as he has taken Mosca, could be tempted by mere gold.

Mosca, however, was present in the first scene of Act I to witness Volpone's greeting to his treasure and in his first speech declared, "Riches are in fortune / A greater good, then wisedome is in nature" (1.i.28–29). The force of Volpone's correction, which begins, "Yet, I glory / More in the cunning purchase of my wealth," was lost on Mosca; and throughout subsequent scenes he naively imagined that Volpone was as much committed to the possession of wealth as anyone else. "I 'am his heire," he says now shortly before the end of the play, "And so will keepe me, till he share at least" (v.vi.14–15). He never dreams that sharing is out of the question for a man like Volpone, who will sacrifice whatever is necessary to maintain his role as fox, masked or unmasked. Thus parasite Mosca, who mistook gold for "poetry," goes down along with one who foolishly dreamed that his masterpiece of fraud could be an end in itself. The fact that Volpone triumphed over the villainous vulture, raven, and crow in no way mitigated the fatal presumption which both enabled him to accomplish that triumph and insured his doom. Volpone's performance calls for the redemptive pardon of a Cynthia or an Augustus; but Venice provides only a Scrutineo with corruptible magistrates in it, and there is no hope of pardon or reconciliation or a conventional comic ending for the play.

Thus the problem of the tone in *Volpone* is due, at least in part, to the limitations of its subject. Comedy, or at any rate New Comedy, requires a social order that is capable of being regenerated, and Volpone's Venice is doomed to go on degenerating like the soul in Mosca's interlude. No one seems to love anyone else there; no one respects another. The merchant leaders have determined that the status of their city shall be wealthy and that her aspect shall continue to be cold, heartless, and beautiful. To make and keep her so, men of their persuasion presumably will go on indefinitely buying, selling, and trading treasure of every common and exotic kind.[28] Venice thus must expect many more purgatories like the one we have just witnessed, all self-induced but none generative of human understanding or compassion.

This is not the usual ending for comedy, but it is probably unfair to compare an achievement like *Volpone* with other comedies—or with tragedy for that matter, even Jonson's own. The timid may take comfort from Jonson's demonstration in Act II of Venice's capacity for gaiety on sunny days and from the character Peregrine's reminders of a world elsewhere with happier aspects that Jonson was shortly to explore in other plays. Some will recognize Jonson's genius in creating and controlling a surface that is manifestly like the real Venice and yet uniquely itself, credible yet bearable as art is bearable and as the three-dimensional world from which art is derived sometimes is not.[29] All great works of art both are and are not about the world they purport to represent, and emphasis on the representational varies from one work to another. In serious comedy and tragedy emphasis is necessarily on the side of the representational, and taken primarily as either of these *Volpone* emerges as a hair-raising comment on life that is effective but, if we ignore the qualifications that hedge it about, misleading.

In the end we shall do well to recognize in this play a work of art that is sui generis, autonomous, and almost self-contained. Seeing it in this way, we may begin to appreciate it properly, on its own terms and with less risk of error—much as we appreciate the astonishing vitality of a pictorial representation of mayhem by Jonson's contemporary Rubens. Indeed, in thinking of *Volpone*, one may usefully call to mind such astonishing achievements as Rubens's *The Hippopotamus Hunt* or his *Prometheus Bound* and note the masterly control that keeps paintings like these from being merely sensational or gruesome. Jonson's claim in the Prologue then tends to become credible, regardless of the explanation we may give for it. "All gall, and coppresse, from his inke, he drayneth," he wrote there; "Onely, a little salt remayneth." In the presence of the genius and control that can make a play like *Volpone* palatable, one can only heed the author and respectfully take him at his word.

CHAPTER FOUR

The Crisis

Epicene and *The Alchemist*

he spirit of Jonson's *Volpone*, regardless of how we characterize it, is far removed from that of his earliest published comedy. Jonson was due to return most of the way to that happier mood with his great *Bartholomew Fair* of 1614; but before that he would write one play, *Epicene*, in which the judgments at the end were unrelieved by anything resembling foregiveness or compassion and another, *The Alchemist*, in which forgiveness, though offered, was in the view of many subsequent auditors and readers offered to the wrong person. *Epicene* was first produced in 1609; *The Alchemist* appeared during the following year. In both much of the folly represented was in the grain, and some of it looked painfully like evil—or so it has seemed to moralistic readers during the past century. In both plays the wicked were among the eventual winners, and in both the institutions of justice were mocked whenever they were not being ignored altogether. Thus Harry Levin has understandably called *Volpone* Jonson's "last experiment in poetic justice" and gone on to say that after this the playwright moved toward an insight achieved by Shakespeare and Donne, "that good and evil, in this world, are matters of opinion."[1] One may agree with Levin's first observation and still question seriously whether any of these three, Shakespeare, Donne, or Jonson, actually came to consider good and evil matters of opinion, even in this world. As regards Jonson, one needs to recognize, first, that the justice rendered at the end of *Volpone* is not only "poetic" but merely "poetic." The wicked are punished there, it is true; but the innocent are not made happy with their rewards, and the institutions that should be counted on to protect innocence in the future are tainted with the same corruption as are the villains they have condemned.[2] Thus the application of justice is threatened just as surely in *Volpone* as it is in *Epicene* or *The Alchemist*.

In none of these plays, however, does the idea of justice itself falter. To borrow Professor Levin's language once more, we may note that Jonson does seem to grow more "genial" as he goes along; but we note also that Jonson's geniality is partly the consequence of where he happened to go.[3] In the first version of *Every Man in His Humor*, in the second and third comical satires, and in *Volpone* he had laid his scene outside England; and in spite of skeptical carping from his critics, he protested that in all his plays he had for the most part avoided being "particular" or "personal" in his representations of human folly.[4] Jonson's protest should probably be taken at face value. His practice in the earliest published works had anticipated and tried to follow the dictum enunciated by a later Johnson that a poet should "examine not the individual but the species ... [and] remark general properties and large appearances."[5] The composition of *Sejanus* and *Volpone* had signaled a minor shift in that practice; for in both of these plays, as has already been noted in passing, Jonson particularized his scene so that they became verifiable as plays laid respectively in Rome and Venice.[6] Thereafter, as he continued to move in the direction of naturalism and adopted the practice of making contemporary London the setting for his comedies, he found himself more and more compelled to come to terms with the complexities of flesh and blood and to temper presentations of abstract good and evil with admixtures of tolerance and mercy. Whether by Jonson's design or by the accident of a choice made for other reasons, both *The Alchemist* and *Bartholomew Fair* required him to deal with follies of the venial order that he had had Downright, or Giuliano, castigate in *Every Man in His Humor;* and both plays thus present a good many amoral characters of the sort that any ordinary unreflecting Londoner might have expected to encounter in the streets and alleyways of the city or at large fairs in the summertime. In earthy surroundings like these Jonson invariably became more tolerant (consider the tone of his *The Gypsies Metamorphosed* and *The Sad Shepherd*); but this does not mean that he lost his ethical bearings. In *Epicene* he dealt with the relatively affluent upper classes, in the privacy of their boudoirs and drawing rooms; and on looking into the motives and practices behind their large pretensions to propriety and rectitude, he found very much to scorn and very little to tolerate. In this play geniality has vanished entirely. One might take critical refuge in the fact that he first let this play be put on by the Children of Her Majesty's Revels at Whitefriars, where the fundamental lack of verisimilitude in performance probably softened the censure implied throughout; but the accidents of a particular production, including the first one, are ephemeral. The text survives to give us some corrosive satire on human cynicism and hypocrisy, and it makes us uneasy even as it makes us laugh. In this chapter, then, we shall deal first with the chilling spectacle of a collapse of justice or ethics in precisely that sector of society where we should normally expect to see it being preserved; and after that, with the paradoxical re-emergence of order at a point where we least expect it.

In one respect *Epicene* may well be the most puzzling play that Jonson ever wrote, though critics have not always thought so. Ostensibly it marks Jonson's complete return to formal plotting after nearly a decade of experimentation. Even the meticulously planned *Volpone* with its balanced elements and its sophistication had an Elizabethan and quite unclassical double plot; *Epicene* by contrast had all the earmarks of neoclassical comedy, as Dryden's praise of it in *An Essay of Dramatic Poesy* has made abundantly clear. "The latitude of place is almost as little as you can imagine," Dryden wrote. "The continuity of scenes is observed more than in any of our plays, except his own *Fox* and *Alchemist*. . . . The action of the play is entirely one; the end or aim of which is the settling Morose's estate on Dauphine. The intrigue of it is the greatest and most noble of any pure unmixed comedy in any language."[7] This was high praise indeed; it was also indicative of qualities that Dryden and his contemporaries would praise in comedy and seek to incorporate in their own plays. Before Jonson's time the intrigue plot had had a long and honorable history, in classical and Italian comedy as well as in English; but in 1668, the date of Dryden's essay, it was on the threshold of its period of greatest vigor, and Jonson's play, by then almost sixty years old, was destined to show the way. In return, Dryden's praise of *Epicene* helped establish a mode of appreciation not only for *Epicene* but for Jonson's work as a whole that was to prevail throughout the Restoration and persist well into our own time.

The model intrigue comedy that Dryden saw in *Epicene*, however, was not entirely typical of such comedy. To be sure, the action is the time-honored one of gulling the old man in order to get his wealth; but the plot that seems to make that action move forward is actually a trompe l'oeil, and the real motive plot—undetected by the audience and by almost everyone in the play except the mover himself—remains hidden until it emerges in the final scene to resolve all the tangles and put everyone in his place. The three principal characters in *Epicene* all have different objectives: Morose seeks to disinherit his nephew and, in order to accomplish that end, goes so far as to make a January–May marriage; Truewit, the nephew's friend, seeks first to prevent the old man's marriage and, failing in that, seeks to achieve a revenge of sorts for his friend by tormenting the old man; the nephew, Sir Dauphine Eugenie, privately pursues an ingenious course of his own whereby he successfully passes off a young boy as a girl, maneuvers his miserly and impotent uncle into marrying the creature, and finally extracts from the old man a promise of wealth in return for release from matrimony—which release he delivers on the spot simply by removing the boy's wig. Throughout the play the members of the audience, too, have taken the boy to be a girl (what, indeed, could be more natural in the Jacobean theaters where all girls and women were played by youths?), so that Dauphine's solution to his uncle's difficulty is as surprising to those watching the play as it is represented as being to everyone else on the stage.[8]

Some critics have turned their attention from the intrigue plot and cited other centers of interest to explain the effectiveness of the play. One, for example, finds interest centering in Morose, his grotesque aversion to noise, and the gargantuan practical joke that his nephew plays upon him;[9] another finds a center of interest in the pervasive theme of hermaphroditism,[10] and still another finds it in the opposition of prose styles.[11] Jonson's dénouement, however, once revealed seems plausible enough; in retrospect at least it does pull the play together, and it has the advantage of allowing him to dispose of the pretenses of all the pretending characters—social climbers, gossip mongers, and the would-be scholar—simultaneously and literally with a flick of the hero's wrist. It is in this collection of characters that a real cause for uneasiness lies; for the London citizens in *Epicene*, without exception, are not merely lazy, stupid, or indifferent, as comic characters frequently are, but are flawed with a moral perversity that seems to be permanently ingrained in the fiber of each of them. Reconciliation among these characters is impossible because none among them is corrigible. The banquet that ought to bring these people together comes at the middle of the play rather than at the end and unites no one. Truewit, whose lynx-eyed perception of the society's follies would have made him an admirable machinator in the simple world of *Every Man in His Humor*, only dimly perceives that the advanced decay of the people in his world has involved him too and reduced his role from that of prime machinator to one of garrulous supernumerary. Like Brainworm he exhibits loyalty to a "master," but unfortunately that master does not need him. Like Downright, also in *Every Man in His Humor*, and like Asper in *Every Man out of His Humor* he seems genuinely distressed at the perverse follies of his time; but he has no effective way to dissociate himself from those follies—no Justice Clement to stand for law, no Queen to stand for sovereignty, no Cynthia, no Augustus. Thus throughout the play he flits from one detail of business to another, seeking first to frustrate the miserly Morose and advance the fortunes of his friend Dauphine and then to discredit his corrupt contemporaries. Yet at the end we see that his whole effort has been like the ridiculous invention of some madman, pretentiously whirling, turning, and buzzing but driving nothing and capable on its own of going nowhere at all.

97

But for the fact that Truewit is not the conspicuous vehicle of the play's thread of anger, he could stand more clearly in line with other angry characters from Asper to Humphrey Waspe in *Bartholomew Fair*. In *Epicene*, of course, it is Morose who has condemned publicly (and obviously with much justice) the cynical, corrupt world about him. But Truewit, in his playful way, condemns that world, too. He makes his appearance almost as soon as the play starts, and he enters with some pointed remarks about the gentlemanly custom of wasting time. When his good-natured friend Clerimont asks, "Why, what should a man doe?" Truewit replies:

> Why, nothing: or that, which when 'tis done, is as idle. Harken after the next horse-race, or hunting-match; lay wagers, praise *Puppy* or *Pepper-corne*, *White-foote*, *Franklin;* sweare vpon *White-maynes* partie; spend aloud, that my lords may heare you; visite my ladies at night, and bee able to giue 'hem the character of euery bowler, or better o' the greene. These be the things, wherein your fashionable men exercise themselues, and I for companie. (1.i.33–41)

The last clause here is revealing. Truewit enjoys very much his place in this society and stands willingly in the very company he takes such obvious delight in criticizing. His game, however, is like a two-edged knife because much of what he criticizes throughout the play fully deserves everything he has to say about it. Thus he continually cuts himself with the knife he legitimately uses on everybody around him. For example, he boasts of his influence on the ladies of the current "school for scandal," who make it possible for him to participate in the social activities that contribute daily to his pleasure and self-esteem; yet he describes them contemptuously (and accurately) as follows:

A new foundation, sir, here i' the towne, of ladies, that call
themselues the Collegiates, an order betweene courtiers, and
country-madames, that liue from their husbands; and giue
entertainment to all the *Wits*, and *Braueries* o' the time, as
they call 'hem: crie downe, or vp, what they like, or dislike in
a braine, or a fashion, with most masculine, or rather *her-
maphroditicall* authoritie. (i.i.73–80)

Similarly he imagines he is able to manipulate the misan-
thropic Morose and does in fact manipulate those two manifestly foolish gentleman Sir John Daw and Sir Amorous La
Foole. With his other close friend, Clerimont, Truewit is
more direct, accusing him, not altogether playfully, of seeking to "destine onely that time of age to goodnesse, which
our want of abilitie will not let vs employ in euill" (i.i.47–
48). He actually begins to preach a bit on the "common disease" of wasting time, but Clerimont laughs him out of his
"Stoicity." "Well, sir," Truewit replies, "If it will not take, I
have learn'd to loose as little of my kindnesse, as I can. I'le doe
good to no man against his will, certainely" (i.i.67–69).

Dauphine is less reluctant to go against people's will than
Truewit pretends to be, but he never presumes to do good to
anyone except himself. Like his uncle Morose he is a confirmed and self-conscious solipsist in a world where self-
interest seems to be the norm. Self-interest is at the root of
much of the pretension and perversity of social behavior in
the play: for example, the outrageous cosmetology of Lady
Haughty and her friends and their preoccupation with varie-
ties of sex (Lady Haughty is said to enjoy dressing Clerimont's page in wig and gown before amusing herself with
him), Mrs. Otter's frantic pursuit of social acceptance in total
disregard of her husband's integrity, Daw's absurd poeticizing and spurious learning, and La Foole's pretensions to

breeding. Yet in none of these does self-interest take the form of withdrawal from society, as it does in both Morose and Dauphine, who are the strong men of the play and respectively its antagonist and protagonist. With Morose the withdrawal is explicit. Apparently he has long managed to shut out most manifestations of the world with the exception of church bells, and these he has avoided by leaving town on Sundays and holy days. Now that the plague and its deaths make bell-ringing a daily affair, he has devised a room "with double walls and treble seelings; the windores close shut, and calk'd: and there he liues by candle-light" (1.i.184–186), communicating with his servant by means of a speaking tube. Dauphine, the would-be heir, effects his withdrawal from society by loving no woman, trusting no man absolutely, keeping his own counsel, and providing his own motive power. The practical reason for this is that his public role as dispossessed gallant must obscure a private action which, it turns out, is the real action of the play.

Whether we should call that action comic is open to question. At best it is probably proto-comic, a manifestation of man's ruthless primitive impulse to survival which the early Greek theater presented sometimes as comedy and sometimes as tragedy and which Shakespeare dramatized in his so-called joyous years in connection with the gulling of Shylock and the humiliation of Falstaff in *Henry IV, Part 2*, and *The Merry Wives of Windsor*. This action is Dauphine's great secret, the full extent of which must be kept not only from Truewit but from all the others in the play and from all those who watch or read it. Thus when Dauphine enters near the end of the first scene and describes his situation as that of a man victimized by a classic disinheritance—his aged uncle has vowed to marry and beget another heir—we all naturally react with Truewit, who races off to assume the classic role of

machinator in the intrigue and rescue his friend. Thereafter
as Dauphine goes quietly about his unseen business of guid-
ing the play forward to its perfectly logical but unanticipated
solution, frantically officious Truewit becomes the man we
watch.

Assuredly Truewit is, as Dauphine says of him at one point,
a man of many plots (IV.v.20). His first plot, unannounced
until he thinks he has in fact achieved his objective, is to prevent Morose's marriage. His procedure is to stand in front of
Morose's house and blow a horn as if he were a messenger
from court. Then, having been admitted, he presents the old
man, for whom the noise alone has been a traumatic experience, with a halter and, holding him and his servant at dag-
ger's point, forces them both to listen first to suggestions of
suicide and then to a lecture of some thousand words on the
subject of women and the danger of marrying them. Truewit's diatribe touches on most of the standard caveats, beginning with what is probably the most ancient:

> Alas, sir, doe you euer thinke to find a chaste wife, in these
> times? now? when there are so many masques, plaies, puri-
> tane preachings, mad-folkes, and other strange sights to be
> seene daily, priuate and publique? if you had liu'd in king
> ETHELRED's time, sir, or EDWARD the Confessors, you might,
> perhaps, haue found in some cold countrey-hamlet, then, a
> dull frostie wench, would haue been contented with one man:
> now, they will as soone be pleas'd with one leg, or one eye.
> I'll tell you, sir, the monstrous hazards you shall runne with
> a wife. (II.ii.32–42)

A conventional warning against cuckoldry ends the list, but
in between we hear of beautiful wives who attract young gallants, ugly wives who tyrannize, fruitful wives who spend
their days thinking of doctors and midwives, learned wives

who demand conversation in classical languages, liberated females, religious fanatics, and patronesses of poetry. Truewit is thorough, and his enthusiasm is unmistakable; but for several reasons we cannot quite call his taunting of Morose normal comic business.

First, although Jonson never allows us to doubt Morose's contemptible aspects, he never asks us to believe that the old man's decision to marry and thus disinherit his nephew, or even his pathological aversion to noise, is totally without warrant. He has already shown us Amorous La Foole in action, and he has let us hear in detail about the kind of society that Dauphine, Clerimont, and Truewit participate in and privately ridicule. Moreover, Dauphine has said candidly to his closest friends, "They are such as you are, that haue brought mee into that predicament, I am, with him" (1.ii.5–6); and even at this point in the play we are disposed to credit what Dauphine says. As for Truewit's diatribe, it contains a series of adaptations, complete with bitterness, from Juvenal's sixth *Satire*;[12] and even if we suspend our knowledge of that fact and assume that Truewit is simply putting together something that will increase Morose's discomfort, we find it difficult to nullify or ignore Juvenal's venom. It describes all too accurately the London society that is being set before us. Truewit, in short, is speaking more accurately than even he realizes and tormenting the old man with a bugbear that is not in the least imaginary but frighteningly real. Two scenes later he will congratulate himself on his effectiveness, saying proudly, "If euer GORGON were seene in the shape of a woman, hee hath seene her in my description. I haue put him off o' that sent, for euer" (II.iv.15–17). The joke is on him. He does not see either that he has failed in his objective or that his objective was a mistake in the first place and might have been disastrous had it succeeded.

Morose, as we soon learn, has not been dismayed so much by what Truewit says as he has by Truewit's penchant for saying too much. So profoundly does the young man's loquacity irritate him that he cries out first, "What haue I done, that may deserue this?" (ll. 46–47) and forty lines later, "O, what is my sinne! what is my sinne?" Absurd as the old man is, we are at this point more than a little inclined to be sympathetic. Dauphine and Clerimont, who enjoys more of his friend's confidence than Truewit does, are not at all inclined to waste sympathy on the old man, but they are both appalled at Truewit's indiscretion and presumption. Dauphine confesses ruefully,

> Now I am lost, I may speake. This gentlewoman was lodg'd here by me o' purpose, and, to be put vpon my vncle, hath profest this obstinate silence for my sake, being my entire friend; and one, that for the requitall of such a fortune, as to marry him, would haue made mee very ample conditions: where now, all my hopes are vtterly miscarried by this vnlucky accident. (II.iv.39–46)

Clerimont is even more bitter and flies into a rage. Moments later Cutbeard, Morose's barber, arrives to report that Truewit's meddling has had the effect of making the old man rush toward marriage rather than away from it; and Truewit, to save face, tries to claim credit for this development too. Clerimont is beside himself. "Away thou strange iustifier of thy selfe, to bee wiser then thou wert, by the euent!" he shouts (ll. 81–82); but the fatuous meddler is undaunted.

In the scenes that follow, down to the very end of the play, Truewit continues to devise his schemes and eventually almost succeeds in driving Morose out of his mind. La Foole is having a dinner party at the house of his relative Mrs. Otter, and Truewit contrives to move the entire celebration over to Morose's house where it can double as a wedding feast, for by this time Morose has raced into marriage with Dauphine's "silent woman" and is looking forward to a quiet wedding night at home. The Ladies Collegiates arrive with their gossiping tongues, imperious Mrs. Otter accompanies them, Tom Otter brings along his collection of carousing cups and promptly proceeds to get out of control, and Daw and La Foole fall into a state of enmity which Clerimont has mischievously initiated but which Truewit with his penchant for plotting manages to turn into a farcical public duel. The cumulative effect of all this business is noise; and to make matters worse, Morose's bride turns talkative and joins the Ladies Collegiates. We know, if we have been listening carefully (see II.iv.85–87), that Dauphine has prompted the bride's shift in strategy here in order to make use of Truewit's unauthorized schemes, but no one else knows that; and Morose, sure that the whole world is in a conspiracy to din him to death, retreats to the top of the house and sits astride a crossbeam (IV.i.21–26).

Morose's agony is not over, however; nor has Truewit finished with plotting. Having, as he supposed, driven the old man into retreat, Truewit now proposes to deliver to Dauphine, whom he considers too independent for his own good, all the Ladies Collegiates as paramours. Morose, meanwhile, is unable to escape noise even at the top of the house and has tried vainly to drive out the intruders with a sword; failing in that, he has raced off to the law courts to seek help with a divorce. This development gives Truewit one final opportunity, and he cannot resist. He will dress Otter as a divine and Cutbeard the barber as a canon lawyer and with false hopes torment his victim still more. Morose is completely taken in by the deception, and once more his anguished remarks tend to elicit sympathy rather than the contempt that one expects to give the "old one" in a comedy. His speech to the two

imposters is the speech of a man who is weary of the world
and wants nothing so much as peace:

> My father, in my education, was wont to aduise mee, that I
> should alwayes collect, and contayne my mind, not suffring
> it to flow loosely; that I should looke to what things were
> necessary to the carriage of my life, and what not: embracing
> the one, and eschewing the other. In short, that I should en-
> deare my selfe to rest, and auoid turmoile: which now is
> growne to be another nature to me. So that I come not to your
> publike pleadings, or your places of noise; not that I neglect
> those things, that make for the dignitie of the common-wealth:
> but for the meere auoiding of clamors, & impertinencies of
> Orators, that know not how to be silent. And for the cause of
> noice, am I now a sutor to you. You doe not know in what a
> miserie I haue beene exercis'd this day, what a torrent of
> euill! My very house turnes round with the tumult! I dwell
> in a windmill! The perpetuall motion is here, and not at
> *Eltham*. (v.i.48–63)

We need to note carefully what is happening here.

In Jonson's plays an absolute rejection of society is usually
indefensible on principle. Nowhere do the plays judge ad-
versely on the healthy bustle of people or the happy noise they
make. Downright, we recall, came close to doing something
like that, as did Macilente-Asper, and had to be "put out of
humor," or at least challenged. Similarly in this play Morose
deserves to be challenged. If only half of what Clerimont and
the young page say of him in Act I is true, he provides a perfect illustration of what Jonson in *Every Man out of His Humor* called a true humor, a pathological imbalance resulting
in monomania—which in Morose's case means a withdrawal
from society. The point to be made here, however, is that
Morose's characterization of the part of London society that

has just invaded his house is only too just; and that part of London society is the only part that the play presents to us. In this instance his distress is understandable. Truewit's baiting, moreover, as we learn at the end of the play, is not really necessary as a means of furthering Dauphine's plot; and even if it were, furthering Dauphine's plot, of which this would-be machinator knows nothing, could not possibly be a part of Truewit's intention. As comic business the baiting of Morose is as questionable here as it was in Act II. Truewit with his "wedding celebration" spinning madly to no purpose is representative of everything in the play that justifies Morose's vexation. Furthermore, as far as Truewit's understanding of the situation is concerned, vexation is the only thing that is happening here. He is consciously engaged in the aggravation and confirmation of a serious humor; and such an enterprise, even in Jonson's comedy, is inexcusable—childishly cruel at best and only superficially amusing.

Morose has at least one other good reason to be distressed. He is under attack by a person of his own blood whom he recognizes as being in no sense worthy to succeed him. This does not mean that Morose is motivated primarily by deep family pride or by some lingering sense of justice. The dominating force in his life, as Jonson delineates him, is his fantastic humor; and in addition to that he is avaricious and might have sought in any case to keep his nephew from inheriting. Still, it would be easier to condemn the man and enjoy the comedy if he were merely a stereotype or if his opposite were less of a "Mosca" at heart. Apparently warfare between the two has been going on for some time, and Morose interprets Truewit's invasion with the post horn and halter as the latest in a series of plots and devices inspired by Dauphine. "This night I wil get an heire, and thrust him out of my bloud like a stranger," he tells Mistress Epicene; and then he adds, "he would be knighted, forsooth, and thought by that meanes to raigne ouer me, his title must doe it" (ii.v.100–103). This last affront to his dignity is what galls him most; for presumably Dauphine's efforts in this direction have at least got him the title,[13] and Morose, now by way of counter-attack preparing to marry at once, gloats for 130 lines over the thought of a penniless Sir Dauphine taking his place with all the other penurious newly made knights in London. The irony of this is that Morose understands and describes accurately (and unlike Truewit, with no intent whatever to deceive anyone) the society in whose estimation Dauphine seeks to be elevated; and he rightly holds in contempt any social order that automatically advances fools if they can somehow buy knighthood, write bad verse, and give dinners. In short, this old man correctly perceives that he is under attack, and he dislikes his attackers with very good reason. He is not simply the avaricious or pathetically lustful "old man" of classical comedy, but rather that old man placed for once in a society bad enough to make him look good. Thus when he goes down an impotent fraud at the end, we wonder whether an impotent fraud like Morose might not be preferable to some of the frauds that seem to be waiting for us up ahead.

Superficially the ending of the play is quite consistent with the aims of conventional "new comedy": the old man is indeed replaced, and youth once more inherits. The difference is that in *Epicene* the spirit of comedy does not survive this conventional dénouement, and the reason for that is fairly obvious. Incorporated in Greek New Comedy and its derivatives are certain assumptions about the persistence of order amidst all the appearance of chaos in this sublunary world, where tragic and comic actions alike occur. In both tragedy and comedy the end for actor and empathizing spectator is knowledge and acceptance: that is, both come to know experientially the way of our world, or some part of it, and, to borrow and modify slightly Stephen Crane's useful phrases, learn that the great death is after all only the great death. Tragedy tends to represent its knowledge as terminal knowledge, at least for the individual at the center of it, while comedy usually gives us knowledge in the context of renewal for both the individual and his society. Both tragedy and comedy, however, involve the removal of fear and offer something like hope or at least peace of mind. A comedy may provide its hope of renewal in one of several ways or in some combination of those ways. In an extreme instance it may suggest that renewal can occur simply as a consequence of the neat working out of the intrigue; this is most likely to happen in comedies where the dénouement can come about as soon as characters have been maneuvered into position where they can recognize one another (e.g., Shakespeare's *Comedy of Errors*). Or renewal may come about fortuitously, as when some magistrate or judge (Judge Clement in *Every Man in His Humor*) arrives like a deus ex machina to set things right, reconcile opponents, and start the wheels of society moving again. A comedy may also get to the point of renewal with the help of a machinator (e.g., Brainworm) who can intervene along the way and keep things running in the proper track. Truewit ostensibly fills this role in *Epicene*, and thus we expect him to be amusing us with clever devices that move the action forward to a proper conclusion for comedy. But Truewit, as we have seen, merely torments the antagonist of the play and does nothing important to further the action, the existence of which he does not even suspect. At the conclusion Dauphine thanks him for his part in bringing forward "Doctor Cutbeard" and "Parson Otter," but for nothing else. No one bothers to forgive Truewit "for the wit of his offense," for he has neither displayed true wit nor committed any offense that is forgivable. He pronounces the "Epilogue" only as a part of the machine, praising Dauphine and Clerimont for activities that in an older comedy like *Every Man in His Humor* would have been his; and he concludes by turning the conventional bid for applause into a suggestion that the audience join in and continue with the tormenting of the discredited old man. By this time we are perhaps prepared to think of Morose as at least as much sinned against as sinning.

Another ironic aspect of the ending of *Epicene* is that its protagonist, Dauphine, stands revealed by his final flourish as the only true machinator of the piece. He is also the protagonist turned deus ex machina, conferring victory and control on himself and crowning himself king of the new order. This is the way of the usurper, the Machiavel, the man of *virtu*, lion and fox, who makes a new game rather than insure resumption of the old. We are reminded of France's Napoleon, who, equally contemptuous of patterns and orderly succession, used a façade of convention to stage that occasion on which he snatched crown from the Pope and made himself Emperor. In any case, no one really laughs here at the end of *Epicene*. The Ladies Collegiates are stunned; Daw and La Foole slink away; the Otters are not heard from. There is no marriage in sight, and dinner has long since grown cold.

Morose is not what is destroyed in this play about "tricking the old one." Once the applause has died down, Morose may even hope for peace and quiet. The real casualty here is the elaborate and ancient house of comedy. In the beginning that house seemed to have all the order and grace of classical architecture, perhaps gone slightly baroque in its old age; but at the end of Jonson's exploration of it in *Epicene* it proves to have been standing upright mainly through force of habit.[14] Undoubtedly the feeling that this lovely structure is pointless is what tempts the modern reader, who may be less inclined anyway to be satisfied with an intrigue, to try to discover a center of interest elsewhere in the play. Ray Heffner's thesis that *Epicene* is built around a practical joke (exposition, planning, execution, and reminiscence) is perhaps the best manifestation of this feeling; but the feeling of dissatisfaction is one which must have arisen in some of Jonson's spectators and may easily have been one which Jonson himself hoped to arouse. In the light of the traditional implications of comic form, Truewit's fruitless performance may appear in retrospect as an ironic memento of a dream of order in a world in which all such dreams of order may seem to have been discredited. To note a final irony, however, the one thing that saves us from what would otherwise be an intolerable nightmare is the uncovering of Dauphine's intrigue. We now know that the society of Morose, Dauphine, and company is at least alive; and where the finality of death is our alternative, we choose life under a tyrant, be he Morose or Dauphine. Thus in the last fleeting moment of the play we see that those ancient impulses which in the beginning produced a social order and gave it meaning and purpose have just manifested themselves before our eyes in something approaching their primitive amorality. If order and the comic artist's witty symbol of that order can no longer celebrate and encourage renewal, then perhaps craftiness armed with a bludgeon may achieve the same result.

Both Dauphine's triumph and Truewit's failure, moreover, help to remind us that the shape of any society is doomed in which men imagine for too long that their sophisticated civility is really anything more than a façade or assume that such a façade can endure without constant human attention to the satisfaction of those primitive urges which civility was invented to make tolerable. In any society that forgets these things someone is bound sooner or later to revert to the post-lapsarian starting point and push the race forward again by committing some of the ancient obscenities. Thus the disturbing thing about Jonson's *Epicene* is not that it is immoral or even amoral but that it reminds us how close we are to our ancestral jungle. The life in this play is the concealed life, the face behind the mask which distorts even as it animates; and that concealed life is the same life that moved the first sentient savage to take club in hand and do away with his aging and troublesome parent. In brief, *Epicene* makes sense not as a demonstration and vindication of the working of a social order, as traditional comedy does, but as a demonstration of the ethical bankruptcy, the essential savagery, of any order that comes to be seen as an end in itself. Having made such a demonstration of contemporary London's callous indifference to ethical standards, it was altogether appropriate that in his next play Jonson should descend to the primal anarchy beneath, where in the midst of primordial rankness he could attempt to build comedy anew from the bottom up.

The actions of Jonson's previous plays had, for the most part, taken place in the upper half of the social structure, that part where human beings presumably make rational evaluations of the information that their senses give them and act more or less accordingly. The assumption in these early plays, moreover, had also been that a genuinely rational action is a moral action; and the presence of a Justice Clement in one of them and good sovereigns in three others had reinforced symbolically the impression of a transcendent moral order. Even *Volpone* had operated on some such assumption. There all the characters at least made a show of behaving reasonably and hence morally, even though most of them were really behaving like animals; and in the end it was a semblance of the moral order which they had mocked that appropriately re-asserted itself to call them all to account for their deceptions. In *Epicene*, as we have just seen, the moral order survived only as a discredited image, an ironically preserved memory of something that once held societies together and measured the morals of their members. Now, as *The Alchemist* begins, we see that London society has abandoned even the semblance of moral responsibility and taken to the country. Plague has come, citizens of means and position have left their places, and the smoky air of the slums has begun to filter through all the fashionable dwellings. In Lovewit's house, where all the action takes place, only the servant Jeremy remains to remind the audience of a life that once pretended to be orderly: and Jeremy, in spite of his assertion that that orderly life will return (1.i.183–188), is capable of reassuring only the most credulous. Clearly he has joined hands with representatives of the underworld and opened his master's doors to them, so that in Lovewit's once respectable establishment the passionate traffic of alchemy and prostitution now prevails. What is even more regrettable, that traffic, discounting a few squabbles between the two confidence men who run it, clicks along with a precision that traditionally has been said to characterize only the way of rectitude and justice. Such is the beginning of the play that Coleridge praised as having one of the three perfect plots in literature.[15]

Not everyone has agreed that Coleridge's praise is well placed. Robert Knoll insists that *The Alchemist* is an intrigue rather than a plot and describes that intrigue as "more a collection than a development . . . a simple situation repeated five times."[16] *Volpone*, however, has this same repetitive character, as to a less extent does *Bartholomew Fair*. In fact, all three of these plays continue the device that Jonson relied on most heavily in his first comical satire, *Every Man out of*

His Humor, and thereafter used more sparingly but always as a device for development, much as a Brahms or a Beethoven repeatedly turns simple variation on a theme into linear development of complexity and power. Knoll himself seems to be responding to this aspect of *The Alchemist* when he writes of the increasing gravity of the problem as it is presented in the successive gulls—from Dapper, who merely wants to win at gambling, to Sir Epicure Mammon, who would extend his dominion over the entire world. And this increase in gravity, or scope, achieved as it is by a series of variations on a basic pattern, might very well be called development, and by some would be called development of a high order. L. A. Beaurline in a recent study has called it "controlled completeness." "The key to it," Beaurline writes, "was the arbitrary limitation of the situation, and the rules for a confidence game. In other words, a restricted field, a set number of persons, and some simple principles."[17] This is a modest prescription, but it is sufficient; and from it emerges a structure that more than justifies Coleridge's high praise.

Since the very sturdiness of *The Alchemist* may seem to some to jar with the anarchy that it depicts so lightheartedly, we may do well to examine that structure in more detail. In order to bring together in one place all the data for his extraordinarily compact intrigue, Jonson resorted to a device that he was to use in the revised version of *Every Man in His Humor* and gave his play two acts of exposition.[18] In the first act he presented his three principals, Jeremy the housekeeper (commonly referred to as Face), Subtle the alchemist, and Doll Common the prostitute, and the first two of a succession of gulls, Dapper the lawyer and Abel Drugger. He also introduced here the broad unifying action for the whole play (largely a submerged action until the end of Act IV) and the first of the two subsidiary actions that hold our attention throughout most of it. The larger action gets passing mention in the first scene when Subtle expresses concern that Lovewit's return may spoil their fun, and Face replies:

> O, feare not him, While there dyes one, a weeke,
> O'the plague, hee's safe, from thinking toward *London*.
> Beside, hee's busie at his hop-yards, now:
> I had a letter from him. If he doe,
> Hee'll send such word, for ayring o' the house
> As you shall haue sufficient time, to quit it.
>
> (i.i.182–187)

Thereafter we are not invited to think of Lovewit until he unexpectedly returns. The subsidiary action introduced in Act I is the conflict between Subtle and Face, already at a lively pitch as the Act begins. Housekeeper and alchemist are rivals for the profits of their joint undertaking, for whatever glory may derive from it, for Doll, and later for Dame Pliant; and trouble between the two breaks out from time to time until Lovewit's return resolves the matter in Face's favor. Act II brings on more gulls—Sir Epicure Mammon and his friend Pertinax Surly, the first of two Puritan brethren from Amsterdam, and an "angry boy" from the country, Kastril, with his sister, Dame Pliant—and it introduces the second subsidiary action, Pertinax Surly's attempt to expose Face and Subtle. Act III and the first five scenes of Act IV constitute the complication or "wind up" (aggravation, if one thinks of the development as analogous to that of a humor or a disease) of the play, and all this takes place without interruption as Subtle presumably is bringing the generation of the philosopher's stone to its crucial point.

In the fifth scene of Act IV the play comes to a climax. At that point Face and Subtle, having amassed a great collection of valuables from their victims, seize an opportunity to pre-

tend that the apparatus for producing the stone has exploded
and triumphantly take possession of the loot. At the same
time, however, Pertinax Surly is now producing evidence to
Dame Pliant that will convict all the scoundrels.[19] He is also
claiming that lady's hand. The two subsidiary actions collide
here as Surly tries to apprehend the two rival confidence men,
but moments later these smaller actions melt into the larger
one as Lovewit returns, takes for himself all the "products"
of Face's wit, including Dame Pliant, and successfully out-
faces the succession of outraged victims, among them Pertinax Surly, as they return to demand justice. The play ends
with a speech by Lovewit, in which the elderly man rejoices
at his luck in getting a young wife, and a speech by Face:

> And though I am cleane
> Got off, from SUBTLE, SVRLY, MAMMON, DOL,
> Hot ANANIAS, DAPPER, DRVGGER, all
> With whom I traded; yet I put myselfe
> On you, that are my countrey: and this pelfe,
> Which I haue got, if you doe quit me, rests
> To feast you often, and inuite new ghests.
>
> (v.v.159–165)

Presumably the ending of *The Alchemist* is as satisfying
ethically as it is esthetically, or so one must believe Jonson himself believed; but scholarly readers of a few generations ago
frequently registered disapproval of what seemed to many of
them to be ethical legerdemain. To these this play, even more
than *Epicene*, testifies to a regrettable collapse of values. Elisabeth Woodbridge Morris, for example, struggled in vain to
find a moral in the play,[20] and Maurice Castelain found the
dénouement morally unhealthy and a serious fault.[21] In our
own time, Edward Partridge, who cites both Woodbridge and
Castelain, explains away the problem by saying that Jeremy-

Face and Lovewit are both convicted by allusions in their own language which connect them with the plague;[22] but this way of resolving the matter leaves us standing with Woodbridge and Castelain and essentially where we were at the end of *Volpone*. The world is as wicked as ever, and Jonson has condemned it again in another ironic comedy, though this time he has not even bothered to bring charges against the most conspicuous offenders. Alan Dessen, calling attention to Face's concluding bid for applause with its address to "you, that are my countrey," declares that Jonson has indeed done something like this and, moreover, has involved his audience in a very special way, setting the play in the fashionable Blackfriars quarter of London and timing it with the plague of 1610, which was in progress even as Jonson was writing; thus by its applause that audience must condone the activities of this "pseudo-Vice," past, present, and future.[23] Alvin Kernan makes a similar comment about the recurring activities of Face and scoundrels like him, but he warns against reading too much despair and sense of frustration into the play: "willy-nilly Jonson's world does right itself each time . . . merely by a defect inherent in vice and folly which leads them to overreach themselves."[24] Overreaching, as has already been noted in this study, is a device that Jonson along with other playwrights had used in his tragedies, but it had long been a recurring feature of the comic theater in characters of various types from Pyrgopolynices to Malvolio.

Kernan's caveat needs to be kept in mind. Some of the somber views about *The Alchemist* are undoubtedly supportable; but audiences, for better or worse, have not been the ones to support such things. Apparently not all scholars would support them either. C. F. Tucker Brooke, who thought *The Alchemist* Jonson's finest play, wrote of it: "Such was Jonson's picture of his neighbors, presented without romance and quite without poetic justice, but also without bitterness. It lacks the harshness of *Volpone* and enforces its moral with a more cleansing laughter."[25] And a recent editor, J. B. Steane, has commented in a similar vein: "Jonson's own creative joy is with his entertainers, and that is no doubt why he lets them off lightly at the end." Steane finds the opposition in the play to be between "a creative vitality that is precious even in criminals, against a heavy, delusive folly that is deadly even in the law-abiding and respectable"; and he adds, "The zest and challenge of the play are in that."[26] One does not have to bypass intelligence in order to sympathize with comments like these; yet bypassing, at least for the moment, what sometimes passes for intelligence can set us on a more fruitful path. All great comedy sits in judgment on the age that produced it, but it does not do that exclusively; and if we are to think of *The Alchemist* as universal comedy and not merely as superb Jacobean satire, we must be able to accept the course of its action and its dénouement as being at least more moral than immoral and consonant with our own notions of fair play. It should appear right to us that Jeremy-Face gets forgiveness while Subtle and Doll get only an escape over the back fence, that Lovewit who abandoned his civic responsibilities to escape the plague should inherit the plunder of rogues who played in his absence and that that same Lovewit should win the hand of the innocent country girl while Surly gets nothing. And all this can indeed seem right to us, as it has seemed right to generations of audiences in the past, provided we can relax our demands that justice be simple, inevitable, and "poetic" and let something more primitive in us—perhaps one might call it "moral intuition"—take over. A child watching the play presumably would react properly—would like Jere-

my and Lovewit and dislike Pertinax Surly—and to appreciate
The Alchemist fully, one must bring to it a childlike response
along with the more sophisticated ones.

For example, a child would probably understand Sir Epicure Mammon better than some of the sober critics have
understood him, for the child can more readily recall how he
himself has taken seriously something as fanciful as Hansel
and Gretel's house of sugarplums and gingerbread or maybe
tried to turn the ocean into lemonade. With the same artless
perceptivity a child might quickly take a dislike to gamester
Pertinax Surly even if that same child should fail to understand Mammon's references to Surly's disreputable activities
(ii.i.9–24). For Surly, whatever else he may happen to be,
calls to mind, if we look at him with our memory as well as
with our intelligence, the practical-minded nursemaid with
her contempt for childish extravagance. The opposition here,
one of several in Jonson's play, is not between folly and truth
but between an optimism stubborn to survive and a niggardly
and cynical refusal to believe that the world can ever be mysterious and honest at the same time or that it can on occasion
be surprisingly gracious. Charlatan Subtle, the mildly wicked
warlock of the piece, who would capitalize indiscriminately
on dreams whether childlike or selfish, clearly thinks of Mammon in a class with generous-hearted children:

> He will make
> Nature asham'd, of her long sleepe: when art,
> Who's but a step-dame, shall doe more, then shee,
> In her best loue to man-kind, euer could.
> If his dreame last, hee'll turne the age, to gold.
>
> (i.iv.25–29)

Where Mammon errs is not simply in wanting something for
nothing but in continuing to dream in adulthood the sort of

lollipop dreams that can be tolerated only in the very young, who are relatively innocent and actually do their dreaming about lollipops. He is not even a greedy and lusty adolescent to be excused on the grounds that he has not yet learned the meaning of satiety. Mammon is old enough to have learned about imposing limitations on human desire, and old enough to know that no paradise worth having can be bought.

Perhaps he does have an inkling of these matters. When Subtle suggests that greed is at the root of his eagerness to possess the stone, he responds with an outrageous lie:

> No, I assure you,
> I shall employ it all, in pious vses,
> Founding of colledges, and *grammar* schooles,
> Marrying yong virgins, building hospitalls,
> And now and then, a church.
>
> (II.iii.48-52)

In view of the wild erotic fantasies he has been indulging in only moments before, the hypocrisy of this short speech almost defies belief. Still Mammon's dreams are not entirely without redeeming features. Even in private conversation with Surly, whom he has no need to impress with a show of altruism, he makes it clear that many of the things he seeks are things he would share:

> I assure you,
> He that has once the *flower of the sunne*,
> The perfect *ruby*, which we call elixir,
>   . . . by it's vertue,
> Can confer honour, loue, respect, long life,
> Giue safety, valure: yea, and victorie,
> To whome he will.
>
> (II.i.46-52)

He would restore *all* old men to youth, cure *all* the sick, and undertake "to fright the plague / Out o' the kingdome, in three months" (ii.i.69–70). Surly, by contrast, thinks that conquering old age would simply mean increasing trade for the London prostitutes and that putting an end to the plague would benefit mainly the players, whose theaters could then remain open. What J. B. Steane has called "Surly's mean-spirited scepticism"[27] is as evident here in his first appearance as it is elsewhere in the play; and it turns Mammon's gullibility and extravagant daydreaming into a highly preferable alternative.

A child might also appreciate Subtle, though modern adult readers seem to have had little trouble taking him at face value. Subtle is Jonson's mage, the farcical counterpart of Marlowe's Faustus and Shakespeare's Prospero, created for an audience that was not going to be asked either to believe beyond their senses or to suspend disbelief. Harry Levin in an interesting short study has reminded us that Jonson's and Shakespeare's two creations appeared in 1610 and 1611 respectively and that Shakespeare had the last word, ironically "sublimating" the alchemist's fraudulent transmuting that had changed nothing.[28] The real irony perhaps is that Prospero's spiritual alchemy itself really changes very little; innocents, monsters, amiable old men, villains, and fools in *The Tempest* come at last to know themselves (or at least some of them do) but remain at the end essentially what they were at the beginning. In a few respects the similarities between Prospero and Subtle are as interesting as their differences; but one major difference overshadows all other points of comparison. Prospero has virtue on his side as scoundrel Subtle clearly does not. A more fruitful comparison for purposes of this study would be one between Subtle and Volpone, also a criminal and a charlatan, who is apprehended and punished for his

activities. These two figures have the same absence of moral
sense, the same delight in their unique performances, and
the same creative energy. If it mattered to do so, one would
be hard put to say which of the two is the more ingenious; but
both dominate their respective scenes to the end, or almost to
that point, and in the end both are undone by less imaginative
men. The great difference between them lies in what they
do. Volpone, to put it crassly, sells a hope of death and invites
men to invest in his own mortality. This is why his victims
are never quite funny in the way that Subtle's are; his Venetian
scavengers all come to feed on carrion. Subtle's victims are
equally greedy, but in varying degrees they all hope for a
miracle. Subtle, in short, asks men to invest in a superior kind
of life, which unfortunately neither he nor perhaps anyone
else can ever expect to possess.

Yet it was a hope of life and not a reminder of death that
Jonson's audiences needed in 1610. No one who had lived
through the summer of 1610 could forget that the background
for Jonson's play included dead carts, burial pits, and weekly
bills; and it is this part of the background with all its chilling
reminders of mutability and human mortality that helps to
make the lighthearted rogues appealing. In the midst of so
much dying these creatures are grasping at what they take to
be means of renewal. Their motives are not lofty, and their
notion of the Stone is perhaps not so spiritual as Subtle represents his own (to the brethren from Amsterdam) to be:

> . . . the *stone*, all's idle to it! nothing!
> The art of *Angels*, Natures miracle,
> The *diuine secret*, that doth flye in clouds,
> From *east* to *west*: and whose tradition
> Is not from men, but spirits.
>
> (III.ii.102–106)

Still, hypocritical pretense nothwithstanding, it has not occurred either to the gullers or to the gulled seriously to condemn life or the living of it. Typical is Mammon, who seriously dreams of having an epicure's heaven right here on
solid earth:

> My meat, shall all come in, in *Indian* shells,
> Dishes of agate, set in gold, and studded,
> With emeralds, saphyres, hiacynths, and rubies.
> The tongues of carpes, dormise, and camels heeles,
> Boil'd i' the spirit of SOL, and dissolu'd pearle,
> (APICIUS diet, 'gainst the epilepsie)
> And I will eate these broaths, with spoones of amber,
> Headed with diamant, and carbuncle.
>
> (II.ii.72–79)

Clearly Mammon is not one to be outdone simply because the
plague is in London or because men die of it. His faith in life,
for all his vanity, transcends the evidences of corruption and
becomes a belief in the possibility of a miracle, even though it
be one wrought by alchemy.

That the plague was still in London when *The Alchemist*
appeared, however, had significance for Jonson's audience
that it cannot possibly have for us. At this distance we need
a more immediately useful measuring-stick if we are to view
the "natural follies," as Jonson said he wished us to (Prologue, ll. 20–24), without a sense of pain or embarrassment.
That measuring-stick, or device of contrast, built into the
action of the play is Pertinax Surly, gamester and companion
to Sir Epicure Mammon. As we have seen, Surly begins by
rejecting out of hand the possibility that he can be persuaded
in favor of alchemy either by his friend Mammon or by anyone else. "Faith, I haue a Humor," he says, "I would not willingly be gull'd. Your *stone* / Cannot transmute me" (II.i.77–

79). One cannot entirely blame Surly here. As a gambler by profession, he makes a living by counting odds. Alchemy—he knows, we know, and Jonson knows—is a fraud, and he correctly sees in the current inhabitants of Lovewit's establishment a collection of rogues, from which he would protect his friend. What makes Surly unlovely is not so much his rejection of alchemy as his reasons for rejecting it. He is like the man who would reject with equal vigor ouija boards, the reading of tea leaves, pennies in the fountain, and prayers for ships at sea—all because such things are of no verifiable benefit. He displays no capacity for childlike enjoyment, no capacity for wonder, and no imagination.

When Surly correctly questions the scientific credibility of Subtle's pretensions as regards the philosopher's stone, Subtle's imagination is more than equal to the challenge.

> Svb. Why, what haue you obseru'd, sir, in our art
> Seemes so impossible? Svr. But your whole worke, no more.
> That you should hatch gold in a fornace, sir,
> As they doe egges, in Egypt! Svb. Sir, doe you
> Beleeue that egges are hatch'd so? Svr. If I should?
> Svb. Why, I thinke that the greater miracle.
> No egge, but differs from a chicken, more,
> Then mettalls in themselues. Svr. That cannot be.
> The egg's ordain'd by nature, to that end:
> And is a chicken in *potentia*.
> Svb. The same we say of lead, and other mettals,
> Which would be gold, if they had time.
>
> (ii.iii.125-136)

The art of the answer here is admirable, even if one is convinced that neither Subtle nor his creator Jonson reserved in his mind any possibility that it might have some truth mixed with it. When Surly finally consents reluctantly to take alchemy as a pleasant fraud ("Somewhat like tricks o' the cards, to cheat a man, / With charming") and cites the language of alchemy as a reason for his judgment, Subtle reminds him about poetry:

> Was not all the knowledge
> Of the *Egyptians* writ in mystick *symboles?*
> Speake not the *Scriptures*, oft, in *parables?*
> Are not the choisest *fables* of the *Poets*,
> That were the fountaines, and first springs of wisedome,
> Wrapt in perplexed *allegories?*
>
> (II.iii.202–207)

But Surly has no conception of poetry either. To him a metaphor is nothing more than a lie under another name.

This is where Jonson, in one of his many strokes of genius in this play, makes his most telling point about Surly—having the gamester, who would not be transmuted by the stone, transmute himself into a Spaniard in order to "trump" the ace-tricks of his opponents. Appropriately Surly is neither changed nor helped by the deception. His incorrigible cynicism is fully revealed when he says to Dame Pliant, who is quite ready to receive a lover and who has been led to believe that the romantically garbed Surly is taking her into the garden for the purpose of proving himself one:

> Lady, you see into what hands, you are falne;
> Mongst what a nest of villaines! and how neere
> Your honor was t'haue catch'd a certaine clap
> (Through your credulitie) had I but beene
> So punctually forward, as place, time,
> And other circumstance would ha' made a man:
> For yo'are a handsome woman: would yo' were wise, too.
> I am a gentleman, come here disguis'd,

Onely to find the knaueries of this *Citadell*,
And where I might haue wrong'd your honor, and haue not,
I claime some interest in your loue. You are,
They say, a widdow, rich: and I am a batcheler,
Worth nought: Your fortunes may make me a man,
As mine ha' preseru'd you a woman. Thinke vpon it,
And whether, I haue deseru'd you, or no.

(ɪv.vi.1–15)

Dame Pliant's "I will, sir," is less pliant apparently than Surly
takes it to be; for she promptly forgets her self-appointed
savior and accepts the hand of Lovewit, brought to her by
Face.

Later the successful Lovewit pronounces her judgment and
his own upon Surly's prudent and economical lovemaking:

Good faith, now, shee do's blame yo'extremely, and sayes
You swore, and told her, you had tane the paines,
To dye your beard, and vmbre o'er your face,
Borrowed a sute, and ruffe, all for her loue;
And then did nothing. What an ouer-sight,
And want of putting forward, sir, was this!

(v.v.50–55)

But we know better. Timidity and oversight have had as little
to do with Surly's losing Dame Pliant as loving would have
had to do with it had he accidentally gained her hand. Surly
loses precisely because he has claimed to deserve the lady by
an appropriate triumph rather than engaged her affections.
His triumph is only a mathematically just one and hence as
hollow as it is loveless. He has discriminated between the lady
and her associates and judged her salvageable, but he has
shown no disposition to embrace her body or touch her lips,
much less respect her humanity. The reformed brethren,

Ananias and Tribulation, who seek Subtle's services on behalf of their exiled congregation in Amsterdam, do not deserve the epithet *Puritan* half so much as he; for Surly in his dealings with "respectable" people is all Puritan, true-blue, and far too good for the lady he fails to get.

In fact, Jonson's "official" Puritans, by comparison with Pertinax Surly, are amusing and sometimes appealing. They are all self-deceived. The devout brethren from Amsterdam would be perfectly willing to make use of whatever gold will buy and, in spite of their pretenses, would get gold by almost any means. Ananias would require the means to be lawful, but Tribulation would settle for success however achieved. A distant relative of these, Rabbi Zeal-of-the-Land Busy in *Bartholomew Fair*, makes similar pretenses to piety; but he, too, manifests human weaknesses, in his honest appetite for roast pig, turkey pie, and malmsey and his lust for willing (and wealthy) widows. For all such moralists, for whom morality is the stock in trade, the risk of hypocrisy, and hence of ridicule, is high. But Pertinax Surly is no hypocrite. He belongs to the same class as intolerant Downright of *Every Man in His Humor* and the unfortunate and vexed Morose of *Epicene*, both of whom display an abstemiousness that is born of contempt and cannot be subverted by appeals to the senses. Surly's kind of denial was for Ben Jonson, always Catholic in spirit regardless of momentary affiliation, a fatal denial, a choice of death as the antidote to corruption; and Jonson invariably gave preferential treatment in his plays to lively people like Jeremy-Face-Lungs and Lovewit. If not showing wisdom thereby, he was at least acting on good instincts. Apparently the Tribulations, Ananiases, and Busys were then, as now, irritating but appeasable, and they provided welcome grist for a comic satirist's mill. The Surlys, by contrast, were men of perennial anger; and the Surlys of Jonson's England were to persist until they had banished the dancing, closed all the theaters, and killed the king. By Jonson's images of men like these we see the face of the real enemy in his make-believe world—whether out on the stage or quietly operating behind the scenes. Call them downright, persistent, or surly—they are all really the same inhuman, incorrigible, unchangeable, anticomic versions of mankind, and the odor of damnation is about them.

The spiritual opposition in this play, therefore, is between Face, or Jeremy, who participates in a confidence game but is still capable of love and loyalty, and the cold-blooded Surly, who pronounces damnation on man's venial sins and pretends to be able to stand above such faults. The background of the conflict includes all those hateful things that any moralist, Surly or not, must point to with scorn and if possible correct—hypocrisy, greed, charlatanism. The background of the background is the biologically dangerous plague, which to the Jacobeans was as symptomatic of moral decline as London's abundance of thieves, frauds, and prostitutes, and which even for us completes the register of perils to which mental humanity is subject. Face quite clearly is guilty of having connived at all this corruption and of having exposed himself to much of it, including the infection of the plague, in his various offices. Figuratively and perhaps literally he is thus contaminated, and his triumph at the end of the play can only be offensive to purists and legalists and lovers of strict justice, who must point out that he deserves only punishment and certainly not the monetary reward or the "I will be rul'd by thee in any thing, Ieremie" (v.v.143) that he gets from his good-natured master. The only answer to such an objection—and it is an answer that is equally useful in connection with the legally damnable *humanum genus* in the morality play, with Spenser's Red Cross Knight (who almost became a suicide), and with Adam in *Paradise Lost*—is that no strictly human being ever really deserves the good he receives, whether that good be Heaven itself or a simple pat on the back. The means of grace and the hope of glory always involve the principle of election in some way, and so here. Face can be saved because he is Jeremy, chosen of his master. He is fully aware of that much even when he strays, and he readily acknowledges as much when his master returns. His greatest joy and honor lie in the marks of his servitude.

Surly's haughtiness, on the other hand, suggests spiritual and intellectual pride. He walks solemnly through the play like one confident of angelic status, pretending invulnerability to the temptations that beset ordinary human beings. It is only fair to say that Surly might very well win in a contest with ordinary humanity—win at least a "moral" victory—if only humanity's lord did not exist or if humanity's lord could be counted on not to come back. The appropriate success story for him would then be something like a truncated parable of the talents.[29] In Jonson's fuller version of that parable Jeremy is the faithful steward who in spite of his faults has tried to keep alive and productive the establishment entrusted to him; Surly is like the would-be steward, who for all his faultlessness, has professed love for his charge and, as Lovewit says, thereafter done nothing. Jonson's Lovewit, moreover, is a lord who is neither dead nor forgetful. He returns to a corrupt world where usury, alchemy, and fornication abound to demand of it such increment as that corrupt world can produce. Like the lord in the parable he has no scruples against reaping where he has not sowed or gathering where he has not strawed.[30] Jeremy, who tricks the corrupt world but is in no sense disdainful of it, has something to show; Surly, ostensibly society's supporter but fundamentally disdainful of everything about it, has nothing at all. The difference between these two defines the set of values that emerges from the play.

Love, respect for place, self-denial—these things are parts of a large complex of attitudes which Jeremy and his master share but which Surly does not. The way of Jeremy and Lovewit is the abiding way of the imperfect world, with its endless getting and begetting in a not always glorious game of acquisition and expenditure, and it is their way that the play ultimately vindicates. Glorious or inglorious, it is the way of fallible humanity, and as such it is preferable to the way which causes Surly to do battle with a laughter-loving rogue and yet remain inactive by preference in the presence of a pretty and willing young girl. Where sterile austerity is the alternative, it were better that Lovewit's house be the bawdy house Surly thought it and Surly himself a whoremonger. Indeed, when Surly declares to Dame Pliant, "where I might haue wrong'd your honor, and haue not, / I claime some interest in your loue" (iv.vi.10–11), we know for certain we are in the presence of one committed to the manipulation of things material and hopelessly incapable of recognizing or dealing with anything that cannot be gambled for, bought, or sold.

Face in the moment of his unmasking also tries to drive a bargain, but he offers love freely, literally and figuratively; and he asks for forgiveness:

> FAC. Sir, you were wont to affect mirth, and wit:
> (But here's no place to talke on't i' the street.)
> Giue me but leaue, to make the best of my fortune,
> And onely pardon me th'abuse of your house:
> It's all I begge. I'll help you to a widdow,
> In recompence, that you shall gi' me thankes for,
> Will make you seuen yeeres yonger, and a rich one.
> 'Tis but your putting on a *Spanish* cloake,

I haue her within. You need not feare the house,
It was not visited. Lov. But by me, who came
Sooner then you expected. Fac. It is true, sir.
'Pray you forgiue me.

(v.iii.80–91)

Jonson gives us no apology for Face, who at the end of the play throws himself upon the understanding and mercy of the audience:

I put my selfe
On you, that are my countrey [i.e., jury]: and this pelfe,
Which I haue got, if you doe quit me, reste
To feast you often, and inuite new ghests.

(v.v.162–165)

Clearly, however, Face is to get no more punishment than the Brainworm of *Every Man in His Humor* got; and we are thus led to assume that the faithful servant will continue to live happily in the London establishment with Lovewit and Dame Pliant.

The fate of his predecessor Mosca in *Volpone* makes an instructive contrast. Mosca, one recalls, got a whipping for similar impudence and afterward a life sentence in the galleys; and comparison of the two moves us to ask not so much why Mosca should have been served differently but how his punishment and Face's lack of it can be included in a single idea of justice. The answer lies in the principle that produced Justice Clement's excuse for Brainworm—"the wit of the offense," which is to say, "the poetry of his mischief." Mosca is as lonely and as sterile as Pertinax Surly; he has no love for anyone, and he betrays the master he is nominally committed to. He betrays, moreover, by prostituting his considerable talents and wit in a scheme to gain control of Venice's wealth.

Like Surly, however, Mosca manipulates only; he never creates. He remains the parasite, as Jonson terms him in the dramatis personae and as the lawyer terms him in the last scene. Mosca's supreme moment comes at that instant when Volpone overreaches himself and is doomed; but in seizing on that instant for his triumph over Volpone, Mosca also overreaches and appropriately goes down with his victim. By contrast, Face's supreme moment comes in Act IV, when in a device of his own creation he undergoes a breathtaking alternation of persons. First, he plays Lungs, the alchemist's helper, to introduce Mammon to Doll Common; then he shifts disguises to greet Kastril, Dame Pliant, and Spaniard Surly as Captain Face. Next he becomes Lungs again to speak to Mammon, and almost immediately Face once more in order to confront Surly in the garden. Finally, as the act is closing, he prepares to assume the person of Jeremy, which is the only one that his returning master Lovewit will recognize. Yet in all this frantic business Jeremy-Face-Lungs never really loses his identity, never employs his talent simply as a means of gaining money or advantage or even praise. What he wins is truly pelf, as he himself says, something got by the way, to be disposed of eventually in a resumption of the game. The game itself is all that counts with Jeremy-Face, and he plays it in the knowledge that he was born to play games and that he serves his game-loving master simply by doing what it is his nature to do. "You were wont to affect mirth and wit," he tells Lovewit (v.iii.80), and Lovewit never denies it. They are well matched.

In the end no one is punished corporally in *The Alchemist*, and no one goes to the galleys or has his ears clipped. The guilty victims simply stand naked, exposed to the scorn of the sportive machinator who has stripped them and whom they no longer even recognize and to the scorn of the audience outside the frame of the play. Surly and the brethren from Amsterdam are no wiser, only sadder. Mammon, appropriately, may be slightly wiser. Jeremy recalls his dream of utopia:

> ... he would ha' built
> The citie new; and made a ditch about it
> Of siluer, should haue runne with creame from *Hogsden*:
> That, euery sunday in *More*-fields, the younkers,
> And tits, and tom-boyes should haue fed on, *gratis*.

And Mammon replies:

> I will goe mount a turnep-cart, and preach
> The end o' the world, within these two months.

> (v.v.76–82)

Thus the play ends with a glimmer of hope that Jeremy's exposure of the fools and hypocrites in his net may lead to small reforms here and there; but it really does not hold that hope high, and it gives no evidence in the plot that any major reform is imminent.[31]

Instead in *The Alchemist* the society that was only tumbling down in the London of *Epicene* here falls finally to the ground and there remains until Lovewit returns to begin to fit the pieces together again. If the play gives us an occasion for optimism (as it surely does), it is in the regularity of the pattern that emerges from all the chaos, in the beauty of Jeremy-Face's creative genius, and in the readiness with which he lays the product (or consequence) of his ingenuity at the feet of his returning lord. One might say that *The Alchemist* encourages us to hope not in the reform of the world but in the unexpected, almost miraculous reconstitution of order and love at the bottom of the heap. In this single pair, who

live by mutual respect (which is to say, love) and not by le-
galities, the play reassures us as *Volpone* and *Epicene* never
pretended to do and as no other of Jonson's plays, even his
sunniest, can do, save his masterpiece of 1614, *Bartholomew
Fair*.

CHAPTER FIVE

Bartholomew Fair

The Metamorphosis of Quarlous

n the year following the success of *The Alchemist* Jonson once again turned to tragedy. This time he brought out *Catiline*, which like its predecessor, *Sejanus*, so disappointed the audience that he promptly allowed it to be published. Soon thereafter he brought to completion another project destined for a better reception, a folio edition of all the work he wished to preserve. *Catiline*, the public failure of 1611, thus was free just in time to become the last play included in that historic volume (which because of printer's delays did not actually appear until 1616).[1] Very likely Jonson put off starting a new play until the summer of 1613; for in September of 1612 he went to France as tutor to the son of Sir Walter Raleigh and remained there until June of the following year. In October of 1614, however, he presented at the Hope with great success his last great play, *Bartholomew Fair*. One regrets that it, too, could not have been included in the *Folio* of 1616, for some consider *Bartholomew Fair* Jonson's best play.

For a long time many have thought of it also as a play distinguished by a mellower tone than that of the other major plays. Alan C. Dessen in his study of the morality of Jonson's comedies cites several who have taken such a view, among them E. A. Horsman, Muriel Bradbrook, and Jonas Barish;[2] but Dessen himself regards *Bartholomew Fair* as an elaborate and pessimistic presentation of "enormities" or abuses which can no longer be checked by justice, religion, or education and thus must eventually spread into the world at large.[3] Another recent study, one by Jackson Cope, also characterizes the play as anything but mellow or genial. Cope calls Smithfield a "seething chaos of a fair," but he suggests that the final effect of "the great humanist skeptic's last great play" is to make it clear that man "can obtain Grace only through the concord of flesh and blood living together."[4] Thus in Cope's view, although man at last finds his only grounds for hope within himself, he does find grounds for hope. Writing more recently than either of these, Joel H. Kaplan has argued for a balanced view: "Smithfield's corruption and depravity are obvious, but are part of an over-all process of revitalization in which rampant energy may be viewed existentially, law made to operate with an extenuating knowledge of human frailty, and art reminded of its true and proper end."[5] Intelligent disagreement of this kind is healthy and long overdue; one would expect a complex play like *Bartholomew Fair* to stimulate and support a diversity of interpretations. At any rate, the one put forth in this chapter is unlike any of those cited in that it includes recognition of the fair's corruption but also presents the view that here Jonson at last was moved to present an imperfect world substantially more conducive to faith and hope than to despair. It also suggests that in *Bartholomew Fair* Jonson found the metamorphosis of his own anger and replaced criticism with acceptance. One may hope that readers will be convinced; but Jonson's text, in any case, is the final arbiter.

The first problem of *Bartholomew Fair* is its structure, and most comprehensive studies begin with that. Ostensibly the action of the play, like that of most other derivatives of Roman comedy, is the ancient game of "tricking the old one"; and the objective of the tricking here is the same as in ancient comedy: to get the old one's marriageable female or his money or both. The plot, however, is unusually complex; and many lines of activity achieve prominence in it. Consequently critics over the years, even when agreeing in their praise of the play's excellencies, have described the structure of *Bartholomew Fair* in different and sometimes contradictory ways. John J. Enck, for example, agrees with Herford and Simpson that the structure is slight and less important than the atmosphere.[6] Robert Knoll writes that the play exhibits a rational orderliness and has "four central intrigues, each dealing with one kind of vanity."[7] Earlier Ray Heffner had found the play unified by the quest for the true warrants or motives for action that lie behind the ones men pretend to have;[8] and Freda Townsend had thought it to be fragmented by five separate actions: the journey of the Littlewits to the fair, the matrimonial and religious difficulties of Dame Purecraft, the related gulling of Zeal-of-the-Land Busy, the gulling of Bartholomew Cokes, and the gulling of Justice Overdo.[9] A decade or so ago James Robinson, in connection with his discussion of *Bartholomew Fair* as a more or less genial comedy of vapors, proposed a new way of looking at the organization of the play.[10] Robinson divided the visitors to the fair into four groups, the Cokes party, the Littlewit party, the Overdos, and the gallants Winwife and Quarlous. Richard Levin has since used the same arrangement as the basis for a more pessimistic view, and some (e.g., Kaplan) seem to consider the structural problem, for all practical purposes, solved.[11] The analysis presented in this chapter, however, assumes a less fragmented arrangement based upon two simple observations: first, that there are two marriageable females in the play, Dame Pure-craft and Grace Welborn; and, second, that all the important activity relates in some way to the disposition of one or both of these. Since both serve as prize in an intrigue of related pursuits and since the victors are entertained in a joint banquet at the end, we may say that the action is at least ostensibly single even though the plot is composed of more than one strand. This much unity, at least, *Bartholomew Fair* derives from its classical ancestors, whom Jonson knew better than most and honored.

The old ones—that is, the gulled ones—in the play are Adam Overdo, who seeks to marry his ward Grace off to his simple-minded brother-in-law so that he may retain control of her modest fortune, and Rabbi Busy, who makes advances to Dame Purecraft mainly because he wants to achieve permanent control over her six thousand pounds and her comfortable home. The lovers who confound these two worthies are Ned Winwife, who begins by challenging Busy and ends by stealing Grace from Overdo, and his friend Tom Quarlous, who seeks no one at all in the beginning but in the end allows himself to be caught by Dame Purecraft. Unlike the young gallants of Roman comedy, however, these two young men win through no machinations of their own or of their confederates but, first, because of accidents that suggest something like providential intervention[12] and, second, because of the susceptibility of their opponents, Overdo and Busy, to a single fatal diversion, Bartholomew Fair itself.

This is where Jonson's last major play makes the crucial departure from its antecedents in Roman comedy and confounds some of the modern critics who have written about it. Almost from the beginning, certainly from the time of *Every Man out of His Humor*, Jonson had been moving steadily in the direction of realism. In the tragedies his concern with verifiable factual detail amounted almost to an obsession, and his passion for verisimilitude was at least noteworthy in the exotic setting of *Volpone* and in the London setting of *Epicene* and *The Alchemist*. In *Bartholomew Fair* he went all the way. The setting for the Induction to that play is the stage of the Hope itself and the time, the time of the performance. The scrivener, reading the author's covenant with the spectators, declares:

> It is further coueuanted, concluded and agreed, that how great soeuer the expectation bee, no person here, is to expect more than hee knowes, or better ware then a *Fayre* will afoord: neyther to looke backe to the sword and bucklerage of *Smithfield*, but content himselfe with the present. In stead of a little *Dauy*, to take toll o' the Bawds, the *Author* doth promise a strutting *Horse-courser*, with a *leere*-Drunkard, two or three to attend him, in as good *Equipage* as you would wish. And then for *Kinde-heart*, the Tooth-drawer, a fine oyly *Pig-woman* with her *Tapster*, to bid you welcome, and a consort of *Roarers* for musique. A wise *Iustice* of *Peace meditant*, in stead of a *Ingler*, with an *Ape*. A ciuill *Cutpurse searchant*. A sweete *Singer* of new Ballads *allurant:* and as fresh an *Hypocrite*, as euer was broach'd, *rampant*. If there bee neuer a *Seruant-monster* i'the *Fayre;* who can helpe it? he sayes; nor a nest of *Antiques?* Hee is loth to make Nature afraid in his *Playes*, like those that beget *Tales*, *Tempests*, and such like *Drolleries*, to mixe his head with other mens heeles, let the concupiscence of *Iigges* and *Dances*, raigne as strong as it will amongst you: yet if the *Puppets* will please any body, they shall be entreated to come in.[13] (ll. 113–134)

And in the promised play, especially in the last four acts of it, the data of Smithfield that emerge from Jonson's language are so convincing that modern commentators, as has been noted, have sometimes found "atmosphere" the most impressive thing about it. Jonson would probably have been pleased with their judgment. In his prologue composed for a performance before the king he began with the following: "Your *Maiesty* is welcome to a *Fayre;* / Such place, such men, such language & such ware, / You must expect. . . ." He took pride in his realism; and these words, coming from him, were a boast, which he was prepared to support, rather than an apology.

Yet a realistic setting for the plot of *Bartholomew Fair* would not of itself have constituted a departure from ancient precedent. Plautus, too, was conscientious about making his references to the life of street and marketplace accurate, though his reason for doing so was probably different from Jonson's. To the Roman writer the inhabitants of the street—going to and fro, buying and selling, plying their trade, making money generally—were mean and contemptible and therefore laughable. Their low background was almost a prerequisite for comedy, and representing that background accurately was thus a part of the responsibility of the writer of comedy. To Jonson, by contrast, the dwellers of the street were at least as good as anyone else and, being less pretentious or hypocritical, perhaps better than most. It would have been possible for him to see the Roman's contempt for common life as something analogous to the Calvinistic contempt for such things on the part of the lower and middle middle-classes of his own day, who made use of the good earth but continued suspicious of it. In any case, being compounded of humble clay and lordly mind, Jonson continued in *Bartholomew Fair* to manifest the proletarian and aristocratic contempt for the Puritanical middle classes of his time and, as in *Epicene* and *The Alchemist*, continued to prefer unapologetic roguery to conspicuous moral rectitude and piety.

The great witness to Jonson's preference is, of course, his re-creation of that evanescent kingdom, the fair itself, with its dust (in spite of the paving that the city gave it in 1614), its fumes, its stalls, and above all its inhabitants. These include a brace of roarers, or bullies—Master Daniel Jordan Knockem and Val Cutting—a ballad singer, a cutpurse, a gingerbread woman, a seller of mousetraps, a costermonger, a corncutter, and sundry others, all professionals and all committed to an objective not unlike that of their respectable counterparts in the middleclass world of business—that is, of getting as much as possible for as little as possible. Several of them, notably one Captain Whit, are bawds, traders in human flesh, and thus are specific counterparts of respectable people like Justice Adam Overdo, the fair's self-appointed scourge, who in his public life has acquired the guardianship of his niece, Grace Welborn, and seeks to keep control of her inheritance by marrying her off to Bartholomew Cokes, his simple-minded brother-in-law. If Jonson prefers these citizens of the fair to whatever representatives of London's more stable world they may happen to resemble, his reason must be that among themselves they make no pretense at being anything other than what they are. With them (and one may believe also with Jonson) the absence of hypocrisy is a virtue. Except when in pursuit of their professions, they are flagrantly rapacious and self-seeking rather than covertly so, and thus they are "honest" citizens of their own world with a consequent penchant for exposing the hypocrite in any other. It is ironic but inevitable that Justice Overdo, the symbol of honesty in respectable London, should be powerless in Bartholomew Fair without the accouterments of his office and unable to set foot in that dusty territory without inadvertently making a show of his hypocrisy to the world.[14]

The undisputed queen of Bartholomew Fair is Ursula the

pig woman, who dispenses roast pork, ale, and beer in her booth and provides for friends and patrons the comforts of a privy in the rear. She also allows the other "Bartholomew birds" to gather in front of her establishment whenever they are not busy at their trades and thus manages to preside over and to some extent direct their various undertakings. The Puritan Rabbi Busy, for all his readiness to condemn, is at least perceptive when he sees in her, more than in any of the others, the power that threatens him: "The fleshly woman, (which you call *Vrsla*) is aboue all to be auoyded, hauing the marks vpon her, of the three enemies of Man, the World, as being in the *Faire;* the Deuill, as being in the fire; and the Flesh, as being her selfe" (III.vi.33–37). Flesh and fire, Ursula herself admits to, as she confesses, early in the play, to the ballad-singer: "I am all fire, and fat, Nightingale, I shall e'en melt away to the first woman, a ribbe againe, I am afraid. I doe water the ground in knots, as I goe, like a great Garden-pot, you may follow me by the S.S.s. I make." (II.ii.50–53). Devilish she is not, of course, except as world and the flesh constitute devilishness. "Body o' the *Fayre*," the phrase applied to her by the young gamester Quarlous (II.v.73), is the most appropriate epithet for Ursula that appears in the play; for she is the fair made comprehensible, its visible microcosm, a mobile compound of flesh and corruption, dust and tallow, fire and sweat, the supreme bawd, mother and queen, friend to most and enemy only to those who like the Downrights and Surlys of Jonson's other plays persist in a denial of their own involvement in her humanity. Thus it is that Ursula's condemnation by the Puritan Busy and Justice Overdo affect neither her person nor her action. She is as morally imperturbable as the earth she represents, while her detractors are condemned in their own self-righteousness.[15] The penalty for their presumption is to make a public recantation, and this they must do before they can participate in the communion of fellowship that concludes the play. None of the three—Ursula, Busy, or Overdo—is at the center of the plot of *Bartholomew Fair*, but they help to define the action which unifies all the other elements of it, including plot. In these three the real plot becomes visible, and in them, though not exclusively in them, it is officially resolved.

The world of polite society to which Busy and Overdo belong includes almost everyone else of importance in the play except the citizens of Bartholomew Fair: John Littlewit and his wife, Win-the-Fight; Win's widowed mother, Dame Purecraft; Overdo's wife, his ward, Grace Welborn, Mistress Overdo's simple-minded brother, Bartholomew Cokes, and Coke's man, Humphrey Waspe; and two young men, Ned Winwife, who seeks to replace Rabbi Busy as suitor to Dame Purecraft, and his companion Tom Quarlous, a gamester. This is the world that supports established institutions, professes respect for law and order, and recognizes ethical values and good manners. Its members live in houses, worship in churches, produce legitimate heirs in marriage, and go to a final rest with gravestones over their heads. Yet while publicly they seem to lead orderly lives, some of these citizens are quite ready to violate their announced principles and engage in pursuits that betray the bestial origin they share with all other human beings.

Take, for example, John Littlewit, proctor, of all these citizens one of the most generous and least tainted with guile, whose house provides the initial gathering place for the fair-goers and whose new puppet play provides one of the motives for going there. So concerned is Littlewit with getting his play produced that despite his expressions of almost uxorious concern for his pregnant wife in the first act he abruptly leaves her in the fourth in the "protection" of two Bartholomew birds, one a horse courser and the other a bawd. Apricot-cheeked Win is even less morally reliable; in spite of her imminent motherhood, she listens intently when Captain Whit, the bawd, tells her that "it is the vapour of spirit in the wife, to cuckold, now adaies; as it is the vapour of fashion, in the husband, not to suspect" (iv.v.50–51), and replies with an enthusiastic, "Lord, what a foole haue I beene!" Mistress Overdo is less naive but almost as enthusiastic in her reception of the Captain's blandishments; and before the play is out, she and Win are both masked and garbed in the traditional green of the prostitute. Dame Purecraft and her suitor, Rabbi Zeal-of-the-Land Busy, avoid such obvious exposures and cannily make their religion serve as a shield for whatever "profanations" their flesh lusts after. Similarly, the two sophisticated young gentlemen, Winwife and Quarlous, equally committed to whatever pursuits seem most likely to lead to pleasure, are conspicuously without scruple, at least for the first half of the play; and they pay only the merest lip service to that code of gentlemanly behavior which presumably distinguishes men of their station.

Some of the representatives of polite society are less blameworthy. Bartholomew Cokes is one of these. An innocent country gentleman brought up to town to marry Grace Welborn, he is so taken with the city and the fair in particular that he spends his money prodigally on everything from ballads to gingerbread and almost drives Humphrey Waspe mad with vexation as Waspe strives vainly to protect him. Waspe by contrast is so disgusted by what he takes to be the unique corruption of London that he loses all discretion and sense of proportion and passionately condemns innocent and guilty alike. In the end both are roundly gulled, Cokes because he does not care and Waspe because he cares too much. Grace Welborn, the ingenue of the play, cares and is cautious, but she is unhappily trapped by circumstances. "Faith, through a common calamity, he [Overdo] bought me, Sir," she tells Quarlous; "and now he will marry me to his wiues brother, this wise Gentleman, that you see, or else I must pay value o' my land" (III.i.273–276). She is unlovely, however, in her self-conscious rectitude. When Winwife modestly expresses the hope that he has earned her confidence, she replies, "I am so secure of mine owne manners, as I suspect not yours" (III.v.298–299). She is contemptuous of Cokes, who is all excitement at the prospect of showing her the fair; and she is contemptuous of the fair. "Truely, I haue no such fancy to the *Fayre*," she says; nor ambition to see it; there's none goes thither of any quality or fashion" (I.v.130–132). Coke's reply is more endearing: "O Lord, Sir! you shall pardon me, Mistris *Grace*, we are inow of our selues to make it a fashion."

Strictly speaking, Tom Quarlous belongs to this group. He has been at Oxford and spent time at the Inns of Court; he walks comfortably in friendship with Ned Winwife, and he moves with equal ease in the company of Mrs. Overdo, Grace, and Bartholomew Cokes. Even so, Quarlous, remains apart from all these. Although a gambler who apparently lives only by his wits, he is reluctant to participate in that fashionable game of deception and counterdeception in a way that Winwife finds perfectly natural; nor is he a contemner of one world as opposed to the other (like Grace Welborn) nor a wild condemner of both (like Humphrey Waspe). He stands outside the categories that Jonson tended to set up even in his most mature plays and so becomes, fully developed, ambiguous, and endowed with credibly human imbalances and contradictions. Occasionally Jonson's characterization in earlier plays had seemed to be moving in this direction, but no character in any of those plays quite achieved the central position in the action that Jonson gives to Quarlous.

The Metamorphosis of Quarlous

The succession of satiric commentators that we have encountered in previous chapters—Downright, Asper-Macilente, Crites, Horace, Peregrine, Truewit, and Surly, especially Surly, all contain anticipations of this final embodiment of the satirist that Jonson gives us here; and, as has been pointed out, critics have often seen in three of these earlier satirists—Asper, Crites, and Horace—a projection of Jonson himself. One notes that these three are all vindicated in one way or another in the plays in which they appear; but *Epicene* did not give us the vindication of Truewit, nor *The Alchemist* that of Surly. One might say that as characterization in Jonson's plays began to transcend the two-dimensional aspect of humor figures, critics of these characters like Truewit and Surly tended to end up discrediting themselves. This may explain why Jonson handled the matter as he did in *Bartholomew Fair*, where the naturalistic context absolutely precludes any simplistic approach to ethical judgment. First, he gave the official function of denouncing enormities or profanations to Judge Overdo and Rabbi Busy, both self-constituted critics and both hypocrites, who end up discredited much as Truewit and Surly did. The activities of these two, however, are only a façade for the real assault on wickedness, which Jonson assigned to two other characters, very different in most respects but both honest men. The less interesting part of this assault he gave to a "flat" figure, hysterical Humphrey Waspe, whose instincts are usually right but whose judgment falters as his temperature rises. The more admirable part, which carries with it an opportunity for growth, he gave to Tom Quarlous, who moves during the course of the play from the vulnerable position of righteous indignation to one of charity. Thus with Waspe holding fast throughout the play and serving as scapegoat at the end and with Tom Quarlous undergoing a change of heart at the center, *Bartholomew Fair* becomes the only play of Jonson's to have a fully realized ethical spectrum. Littlewit's trip to the fair provides the plot that holds everything together. Waspe shows the presumptuous posture that Quarlous manages to escape. Busy and Overdo in their transition from hypocritical castigation to repentance serve to illuminate the course of the emerging and enveloping action. In Quarlous that action finds full and conspicuous embodiment, and by his presence the play achieves a distinctive unity of its own. In him, moreover, Jonson's exploration of the liability of the satiric commentator comes to an end.[16]

Quarlous's part spans almost the entire scope of the play. We first hear him mentioned early in the first scene, as the Littlewits, John and Win-the-Fight, are explaining to Ned Winwife that their widowed mother, whom Ned is seeking to marry, is now being pursued by an old elder from Banbury (Rabbi Busy). She herself, they add, is pursuing a fictitious madman whom some fortune-teller has said she must marry within the week; and they advise Winwife to take lessons in madness from his madcap friend Quarlous if he would displace Rabbi Busy and capture the widow for himself. Shortly thereafter Quarlous enters and promptly proves his "madness" by plunging straightway into a kissing flirtation with Win Littlewit, who is pretty and dressed for a party but also married to John Littlewit, present, and conspicuously pregnant. The flirtation, it turns out, was Littlewit's idea, planned with a view to conditioning his wife to the ways of sophisticated tavern society, which he as a would-be poet and playwright expects shortly to join; and Quarlous, though he enjoys the kissing, considers Littlewit no wiser than his name for wanting it to continue.

Quarlous's real purpose in coming to Littlewit's house apparently is to find and rebuke Winwife, whom he considers guilty of a much greater folly in continuing to pursue a widow,

Dame Purecraft. The speech that he proceeds to deliver on this subject is one of Jonson's best and also one of his most scurrilous. It runs, in part, as follows:

> I'faith, would thou wouldst leaue thy exercise of widdow-hunting once! this drawing after an old reuerend Smocke by the splay-foote: There cannot be an ancient *Tripe* or *Trilli-bub* i' the Towne, but thou art straight nosing it, and 'tis a fine occupation thou'lt confine thy selfe to, when thou ha'st got one; scrubbing a piece of Buffe, as if thou hadst the perpetuity of *Pannyer-alley* to stinke in; or perhaps, worse, currying a carkasses, that thou hast bound thy selfe to aliue. I'll be sworne, some of them, (that thou art, or hast been a Suitor to) are so old, as no chast or marryed pleasure can euer become 'hem: the honest Instrument of procreation, has (forty yeeres since) left to belong to 'hem, thou must visit 'hem, as thou wouldst doe a *Tombe*, with a Torch, or three hand-fulls of Lincke, flaming hot, and so thou maist hap to make 'hem feele thee, and after, come to inherit according to thy inches. A sweet course for a man to waste the brand of life for, to be still raking himselfe a fortune in an old womans embers; we shall ha' thee, after thou hast beene but a moneth marryed to one of 'hem, looke like the *quartane ague,* and the black *Iaundise* met in a face, and walke as if thou had'st borrow'd legges of a *Spinner,* and voyce of a *Cricket.* (1.iii.62–83)

In spite of scurrility this speech is fraught with moral indignation, and it alone would put Quarlous in the company of Asper and Surly; but he confirms his position there within the next fifty lines or so by delivering a similar speech on the subject of Rabbi Busy:

> A notable hypocritical vermine it is; I know him. One that stands vpon his face, more then his faith, at all times; Euer in seditious motion, and reprouing for vaineglory: or a most

lunatique conscience, and splene, and affects the violence of *Singularity* in all he do's: (He has vndone a Grocer here, in Newgate-market, that broke with him, trusted him with Currans, as errant a Zeale as he, that's by the way:) by his profession, hee will euer be i' the state of Innocence, though; and child-hood; derides all *Antiquity;* defies any other *Learning,* then *Inspiration;* and what discretion soeuer, yeeres should afford him, it is all preuented in his *Originall ignorance;* ha' not to doe with him: for hee is a fellow of a most arrogant, and inuincible dulnesse, I assure you. (I.iii.135–148)

Thereafter he stands by, observing the entry of Bartholomew Cokes and company, who have come to get the marriage license that Littlewit as proctor has prepared for Cokes and Grace Welborn, and comments that Grace is ill matched with such a dolt. With Winwife he decides to follow Cokes's party to the fair and see what "creeping sport" these "flies" will engender on an August afternoon.

Up to this point we can only take Quarlous at face value. He is well bred, well educated, intelligent, and acid tongued. Quite clearly he is contemptuous of John Littlewit, Bartholomew Cokes, and Rabbi Zeal-of-the-Land Busy, and only slightly less contemptuous of his friend Winwife. Still like any other young gentleman he can join in the pursuit of a pretty girl when the girl is as pretty as Grace. In spite of his reference to "flies," Grace is obviously one of his motives for being willing to strike out for the fair when the Three Cranes, the Mitre, or the Mermaid would normally be much more to his liking. His attitude toward the fair becomes clear almost as soon as he arrives there. Naturally both young men try to push aside the vendors that cluster about them, but whereas Winwife's rejection of the Bartholomew birds is relatively straightforward, Quarlous's method includes both a sarcastic tone and

a free use of classical allusions that can only make them wonder with what new sort of knives he is cutting them. To the
hobbyhorse seller (that is, the toy seller) he cries "S'lid! heere's
Orpheus among the beasts, with his Fiddle, and all!" And to
Joan Trash, the gingerbread woman, he says, "*Ceres* selling
her daughters picture, in Ginger-worke" (ii.v.8–12). This is
why we cannot be greatly impressed when he addresses Ursula at her entrance with "Body o' the *Fayre!*" The phrase is
apt, but the voice has a sneer in it. Besides the rest of the line
is as follows: "What's this? mother o' the Bawds?" (ii.v.73–
74). When Winwife tries to enter the fun with a classical al-
lusion of his own ("Mother o' the *Furies*, I thinke, by her
firebrand"), Quarlous shifts the rules of his word game: "Nay,
shee is too fat to be a *Fury*, sure, some walking Sow of tallow!"

The real test comes when Dan Jordan Knockem, the horse
courser, accosts them and loudly invites them to drink with
him at Ursula's. Winwife is for avoiding the encounter, but
Quarlous forces it—not, however, because he possesses the
common touch. As the drinking proceeds, it becomes clear
to us—and eventually to Jordan, Ursula, and young Mooncalf,
who is helping to serve—that Quarlous drinks with common
people to see how far he can go in heaping abuse on them
before they take him seriously enough to begin fighting. This
time he goads Ursula into making some choice remarks about
"leane playhouse poultry": "I, I, Gamesters, mocke a plaine
plumpe soft wench o' the Suburbs, doe, because she's iuicy
and wholesome: you must ha' your thinne pinch'd ware, pent
vp i' the compasse of a dogge-collar, (or 'twill not do) that
lookes like a long lac'd *Conger*, set vpright, and a greene
feather, like fennell, i' the Ioll on't" (ii.v.83–88). Still, it is
Quarlous who finally strikes the first blow, followed immediately by Jordan and eventually Ursula with her dripping

pan. Ursula, fortunately for Quarlous and Winwife, stumbles and scalds her leg with the hot grease, and they make their escape.

In Act III Quarlous embarks on a project that, in effect, unites him with the people of the fair. During the first part of that act he walks about as before, observing and commenting superciliously, until finally he sees Ezechiel Edgworth, a clever young cutpurse, relieve Bartholomew Cokes of his money. Waspe in exasperation seizes the box with the marriage license in it and holds it for safekeeping, but Quarlous holds Edgworth:

> QVAR. Doe not deny it. You are a cutpurse, Sir, this Gentleman here, and I, saw you, nor doe we meane to detect you (though we can sufficiently informe our selues, toward the danger of concealing you) but you must doe vs a piece of seruice.
>
> EDG. Good Gentlemen, doe not vndoe me; I am a ciuill young man, and but a beginner, indeed.
>
> QVAR. Sir, your beginning shall bring on your ending, for vs. We are no Catchpoles nor Constables. That you are to vndertake, is this; you saw the old fellow, with the blacke boxe, here?
>
> EDG. The little old Gouernour, Sir?
>
> QVAR. That same: I see, you haue flowne him to a marke already. I would ha' you get away that boxe from him, and bring it vs. (III.v.236–250)

Both Edgworth and Quarlous are telling the truth. Edgworth is "but a beginner, indeed," and Quarlous is truly neither catchpole nor constable. In fact, Quarlous here joins the forces of lawlessness when he takes Edgworth's relatively simple knavery and pushes it in the direction of evil, making him a cutpurse for hire—or, worse, he puts the young man in the hateful position of stealing under threat of blackmail. Moreover, while one of Quarlous's motives may be to rescue Grace Welborn, he acts on an equally strong and perhaps even stronger motive: to turn the tables on Adam Overdo and grab Grace's inheritance for himself.

The extent of Quarlous's corruption becomes clear in Acts IV and V. In Act IV Mistress Grace discovers the consequences of confiding in the two gentlemen: both are now pursuing her, with swords drawn and ready to fight for her hand. The irony of the situation is that Winwife, long given to pursuing widows for their wealth, is now pursuing an unmarried young woman for love alone, while Quarlous by contrast is now guilty of the same cynicism that in varying degrees has corrupted Littlewit, Busy, Overdo, and up to this moment Winwife. Admittedly the guilt in Quarlous does seem less ingrained than that in some of the others, for he accepts Winwife's triumph in Act V without bitterness and lets Grace go. Nevertheless the unsavory motive remains. Turning to that same Dame Purecraft who prompted his scurrilous remarks to Winwife in Act I, he observes cynically: "It is money that I want, why should I not marry the money, when 'tis offer'd mee? I haue a *License* and all, it is but razing out one name, and putting in another. There's no playing with a man's fortune" (v.ii.80–84). For the moment at least, Quarlous identifies himself with avaricious humanity and declares it a principle, that where money is concerned, human values must give way.

Thus the play reaches a point at which four of the male principals, and those the four most important, are trapped in a destructive pursuit of self-advancement. Three of them cloak their pursuits in a public show of respectability; Busy

151

calls his pursuit religion, Overdo calls his reform, and Littlewit calls his poetry. Quarlous, to say the least, does not lie to
himself. "It is money that I want," he says; but he is engaged
in a quest that is just as reprehensible as those of the others,
and his objective is actually identical with Busy's. Moreover,
all four men are engaged in one way or another in the exploitation of the opposite sex. They are grasping rather than giving, using rather than serving; and not one of them gives any
evidence of will or power to reverse himself. Consequently
Jonson's plot requires at this point the introduction of a cata-
lyst, a deus ex machina of some kind—an agent of grace, some
might call it—whereby the series of reformations necessary
to comedy can begin.

The agent who fills this need in *Bartholomew Fair* is a
madman, Troubleall, who, we are told, has been haunting
the fair with one persistent question, "Have you warrant for
what you do?"[17] We learn further that the man was a minor
official in the court of pie pouldres (set up to settle disputes
at the fair) and that Overdo a year or so before the time of the
play removed him from his position. Since then brooding
over loss of place has driven the poor fellow out of his wits,
and he will do nothing without a "warrant" from Justice
Overdo—or almost nothing, for Grace Welborn asks him to
choose between the names that rivals Winwife and Quarlous
have written down on a blank tablet, and Troubleall decides
in favor of Winwife. By this, for him, exceptional act he becomes the "ragged prophet" (Quarlous's terms) thrust in
their way by Destiny, which, as Grace says, "has a high hand
in businesse of this nature" (iv.iii.51–52).[18] But because she
will not at first tell which of the two suitors Destiny has thus
chosen, Quarlous lures Troubleall into Ursula's booth, steals
his clothes, and in that disguise takes a "second look" at
Grace's tablet. In this way he learns that as far as winning

Grace Welborn is concerned, Destiny has passed him by. Yet disguised as Troubleall he is now a madman and the natural objective of Dame Purecraft's quest. He is also in line to receive the blank warrant that a conscience-troubled Justice Overdo issues in order to soften the distress of a wretch whom he has inadvertently driven out of his mind. Thus with a blank warrant at his disposal and the wit to use it, Quarlous is in a position to bilk Overdo of his money and, having also gained possession of Coke's marriage license, to make or break a marriage with Grace Welborn as well.

That Quarlous does none of these things—or none to anyone else's detriment—must be put down simply as a mystery of the play and a testament to Jonson's good sense, certainly a testament to his respect for realism in the theater. If it must be argued that Quarlous married the widow for money, it must also be noted that by ignoring the madman's mark in Grace's book he could have had money and a young and pretty wife as well. The young man's change here is, like most changes of heart, without palpable motivation; yet by its very capriciousness it is credible. It forms a pattern with all the things that are generous, honest, and more or less capricious in this play, the wide-eyed eagerness of the Littlewits to visit the fair (quite apart from John's interest in presenting his literary effort there), the naiveté which prompts both Littlewits to believe that life in literary circles is perennially innocent and gay, the persistence of honor and compassion for one another among the thieves of Bartholomew Fair, Overdo's compassion for Troubleall, Busy's appetite for food (however much he may be ashamed of it), the ladies' interest in sex. Capriciousness is the element of change that saves limited man from the state determined by his human condition. Without some such element in life—call it capriciousness, wilfulness, or even error—everyone would necessarily remain the prisoner of his physical constitution; no man could ever escape the tyranny of his humor.[19] "Some falls," says Lucius in Shakespeare's *Cymbeline*, "are means the happier to arise" (IV.ii.403). More to the point, Mariana observes in *Measure for Measure:*

> They say best men are moulded out of faults,
> And, for the most, become much more the better
> For being a little bad.
>
> (V.i.444–446)

This is the optimistic principle at work in Jonson's *Bartholomew Fair*, where the germ of change is endemic in the smelly air and dust of the place from which the play takes its name; and much of the change that occurs, particularly at the end, gives us a faint and unheroic echo of the fortunate fall.

This is not to suggest that the dust of Smithfield has anything especially miraculous about it. People there are as wicked as they are anywhere else, as Jonson's portrayal of the fair makes quite clear.[20] The difference is that the denizens of that place do not delude themselves about who or what they are. Everything they do begins in self-acceptance, and their fundamental honesty is infectious. People who are "caught" by this aspect of the fair are usually the better for it. Thus Rabbi Busy finally succumbs to the "sinful" temptation of theater only to come to better knowledge when the puppet performers in Littlewit's absurd play meet his charges by proving that they are neither male nor female and show, moreover, that they speak with as much "inspiration" (indeed, how else could puppets speak?) as anyone. "Let it goe on," he says, "For I am changed, and will become a beholder with you!" (V.v.156–157). Littlewit stupidly lets his wife drift toward prostitution; but when she reaches that point (at least technically), he comes quickly to the essential knowledge that she is not simply "little wife . . . little pretty *Win*" but a woman of flesh and blood. Thus he profits. Similarly, Justice Overdo's series of denunciations leads him inevitably to the condemnation of another lady in prostitute's green, who turns out to be his own wife, Mistress Alice Overdo. Quarlous is a witness to all these salutary humiliations and enlightenments, the cumulative implication of which is that many kinds of men may be brought to wisdom through the exercise of folly. Then suddenly his own humiliation is upon him as the real Troubleall returns clad only in Ursula's dripping pan. Thus he, too, stands exposed by fortune's accidents along with all those weaker fools from whom he has tried by exercise of superior wit to dissociate himself.

From here there is no way out but up; and strength of wit, with perhaps character added, makes it appropriate and possible for Quarlous to lead the way. Paying his respects to the madman Troubleall and thanking him for the gift of a good wife, he invites Overdo to use his authority and means and make a proper comedy of the day's mistakes: "Stand not you fixt here, like a stake in *Finsbury* to be shot at, or the whipping post i' the *Fayre*, but get your wife out o' the ayre, it wil make her worse else; and remember you are but *Adam*, Flesh, and blood! you haue your frailty, forget your other name of *Ouerdoo*, and inuite vs all to supper" (v.vi.93–98). And Overdo is responsive to the suggestion. Reaching down and taking in hand the despondent Waspe, whose chagrin has all but reduced him to silence ("I will neuer speak while I liue, againe, for ought I know"), he speaks reassuringly, "Nay, *Humphrey*, if I be patient, you must be so too; this pleasant conceited Gentlemen hath wrought vpon my iudgement, and preuail'd" (v.vi.105–107).

The reduction of the angry critic—for anger has been an aspect of all the satirical commentators in previous plays, from

Asper to Surly—to a mere Waspe who can be mollified thus by human persuasion is a part of the triumph of this play and possibly a part of Jonson's triumph over himself. Similar characters in the other plays of Jonson's middle period had simply abandoned society or expressed incorrigible contempt for it. One calls to mind that Shakespeare's middle plays exhibit parallel examples: witness Malvolio's, "I'll be reveng'd on the whole pack of you,"[21] and Iago's bitter, "From this time forth I never will speak word."[22] Until *Bartholomew Fair* Jonson's solution was no better. Surly's farewell in *The Alchemist* is representative:

> Must I needs cheat my selfe,
> With that same foolish vice of honestie!
> Come let vs goe, and harken out the rogues.
> That FACE I'll marke for mine, if ere I meet him.
>
> (v.v.83–86)

But Shakespeare in the end brought his morally indignant Prospero to express a patient tolerance for a very different kind of angry man with "this thing of darkness / I acknowledge mine."[23] So Overdo accepts his angry Waspe. So, too, one should add, does the acid-tongued Quarlous seem to recognize the beauty of young love and lay hold on the hope that regenerative love may make a blessing even of his union with aging Dame Purecraft; for in the end he uses the warrant to free Grace Welborn to accept the embrace of his rival, and he takes the purloined license to clear the way for his own permanent union with the despised widow.

The metamorphosis of Quarlous helps us get into focus the fact that *Bartholomew Fair* itself is a metamorphosis, or rather that it represents the completion of a metamorphosis that began when Jonson grew dissatisfied with his early imitations of Roman comedy and threw overboard his skill at tight plotting. Time has shown that his earliest attempts to transform traditional dramatic structure were abortive; but the attempts continued, as experiments in tragedy conditioned the tone of *Volpone* and *Epicene* and as the moral ambiguity of the latter carried over into *The Alchemist*. Form achieved its fulfillment in those plays of 1606, 1609, and 1610. In the last two of them, moreover, Jonson learned to do without the contrasting parallel plot that distracts modern readers of *Volpone* and produced plays that even critics like Dryden and Coleridge could praise without reservations. Yet up to this point Jonson had not succeeded in accommodating satisfactorily in a comic action his ubiquitous castigator, always a serious character, replete with righteousness and deeply offended by the spectacle of human folly. Whether Jonson had seen the problem as a continuing one or not is debatable, but the problem was real enough. Moral indignation, whatever we may think of it, is inevitably a consequence of human pride or human folly or perhaps both; and Jonson before *Bartholomew Fair* had always dealt rigorously with it, creating the condemner to condemn and then frequently punishing him or threatening to punish him for performing his office. The temporary solution of *Every Man out of His Humor*, a sovereign's gracious touch, could not really be repeated after the mode of comical satire had proved to have only limited usefulness. The viable solution came, as we have now seen, with the division of the role between Quarlous and Waspe, the one to be transformed as a consequence of his full participation in the human comedy and the other to be urged to participate at least in the feast of reconciliation with all the others, forgiving and forgiven.

Some might say that this division in role was simply another aspect of the tendency of Jonson's last great play to dissolve into fragments, with multiple actions, strings of episodes, and character after character crowded into the canvas to create an illusion of festive business. The diversity exhibited in *Bartholomew Fair* has certainly bewildered scholars and critics and may have caused it to be the least frequently performed of all Jonson's major plays; but it should not, and does not in the best recent criticism, obscure the skill with which Jonson has organized his various activities and threads of plot into one fabric, one design, and one action, all preparing us for the exhortation at the end, "remember you are but *Adam*, Flesh and blood! you haue your frailty."[24] Comprehensive as it is, the perspective of the play is still too narrow in its focus to offer more than a hint of humanity's vast range; but it is not weak or careless in its plotting, and it exhibits something of the complexity, the contradictions, and the excitement of any scene that captures the true stir of vital humanity.

In short, the integrity of plot which Jonson achieved in his second version of *Every Man in His Humor*, *Epicene*, and *The Alchemist* is in this play too. For all its complexity it still has the firm shape of Roman comedy, and it celebrates the same natural succession of youth to the fortunes and prerogatives of age. The difference is that Jonson's play temporarily relieves that ancient pattern of its monotony of perpetual recurrence by mating not only two young lovers with one another but a youthful Quarlous with an aging Dame Purecraft. One can argue that this January–May solution in reverse can hardly have modified the mode and practice of popular comedy; for that kind of comedy has continued essentially unaltered since Jonson's day, celebrating from one generation to the next that process by which civilization renews itself and will probably continue so to flourish as long as civilization itself survives. Yet in the impending marriage of Quarlous and Dame Purecraft with which *Bartholomew Fair* ends there is a suggestion that bright youth as well as age can stoop to folly, that being reconciled to the old one may be at least as good as tricking him, and that in such comprehensive unions we may find our best hope of heaven. At any rate, in the world of Jonson's plays the routine achievement of heaven's bliss in the beloved's arms is seldom more than an adolescent's cliché and hardly worth making the end and objective of a dramatic argument.

CHAPTER SIX

Epilogue

A Tale of a Tub

artholomew Fair was Jonson's last significant success in the public theater. Years of high public esteem, great productivity, and influence still lay ahead. He was yet to bring out the great collected edition of 1616, the shorter collection of three plays in 1631,[1] and several quartos; he was to write much fine poetry and some of his better masques; but the plays to come, five of them if one counts A Tale of a Tub, were all to be failures. The Devil Is an Ass (1616), an uneven piece, for some reason drew the displeasure of the King. The Staple of News (1626), The New Inn (1629), and The Magnetic Lady (1632) failed at their first performance. A Tale of a Tub, which may have been a much older play revised and revived, was performed at the Cockpit in 1633, apparently with enough success to justify a performance at court in January of 1634; but there it was "not likt," and there is no record of further performances.[2] Although Dryden's observation in the Essay of Dramatic Poesy that these last plays of Jonson's "were but his dotages"[3] is perhaps too sweeping, subsequent criticism has tended to support it. The most substantial effort to compel a reconsideration of the matter is that by Larry S.

Champion in his study *Ben Jonson's "Dotages."* Champion excludes *A Tale of a Tub* as being early work but argues that the other plays should be read as "attempts to revivify satiric comedy and to broaden its appeal through adaptation of aspects of the native dramatic tradition."[4] The point is convincingly made, though one may still question whether such attempts—if attempts they were—were well advised. Why after *Bartholomew Fair* should Jonson abandon his hard-won territory and return to the less exciting terrain of comical satire—comical satire, moreover, without the exciting figure of the satirist to enliven it? *The Devil Is an Ass* can be excused, perhaps, as an understandable relaxation after the major achievement of its immediate predecessors. But what of the three that he wrote between 1626 and 1632? Are these reversions, departures, or simply products of a decline?

There can, of course, be no final answer to such questions, but several possibilities suggest themselves. For one thing, ten years elapsed between *The Devil Is an Ass* and *The Staple of News,* and during that time Jonson wrote no plays at all. He returned to the theater ten years older and ten years out of practice. To this extent there was certainly decline. Jonson's London, however, was different too. It was an increasingly Puritan London; and his sovereign was no longer the crusty, comfortable friend Jonson had found in James but an elegant precisian, though no Puritan, with little taste for Jonson's lusty brand of classicism. One hesitates to accept the view that Jonson's last works were reversions to or continuations in the main stream of his talent, whether that main stream be thought of as satire, morality, or allegory.[5] There was a departure of some sort in the work that Jonson wrote for the theater of Caroline London, but one must allow for the possibility that the departure was a carefully considered one and that Jonson thought he was meeting a new audience on its own terms. *Volpone, Epicene,* and *The Alchemist* were all continuing to have performances from time to time in those years, but *Bartholomew Fair* was not performed, or at least there is no record that it was. Jonson if he wished to build on the achievement that *Bartholomew Fair* may well have represented for him had no reason to believe that by continuing to write of "Adam, flesh and blood" he would be producing anything but closet drama. Thus with high hopes but with the same blindness that once led him to imagine that *Sejanus* and *Catiline* would be popular as tragedies, he wrote those intellectually edifying pieces that seem to have bored most people and pleased almost no one.

Two pieces that he may have written during this period are exceptions. One is *The Sad Shepherd,* that tantalizing fragment of romantic pastoral found among Jonson's papers after his death.[6] No one could be bored with this work, but Jonson left it unfinished. The other is *A Tale of a Tub,* a play that Jonson seems to have revived expressly to turn it into an attack on Inigo Jones.[7] There is no external evidence to date the play, and many historians tend to place it with his very earliest things, even before *The Case Is Altered,* which was written in 1598 or thereabouts.[8] Robert E. Knoll so places it and argues that the play is thoroughly Elizabethan in conventions and tone.[9] So it is, in the sense that *Bartholomew Fair* is Elizabethan; but it also bears the same kind of relation to Roman comedy that *Bartholomew Fair* bears. All the conventional marks of Roman comedy are there: a careful observance of the unity of time and a reasonably close observance of the unity of place; a group of familiar stereotypes, among them an amiably rebellious son, gulled parents, wily servants, and a mischief-maker; an intrigue plot with disguises and cases of mistaken identity. In addition to these particulars it has the domestic setting common in New Comedy generally, and it ends with marriages and a feast of reconciliation.

C. H. Herford, who thought the play a good example of good early work summed up his view as follows: "His classical discipline asserts itself unmistakably; in no English play up to this date had the Unities been so approximately observed as in this comedy of country-folks and clowns, and very few could offer a plot so well traced, coherent, and so free from the idleness which Hamlet was justly to rebuke in the bulk of the plays of his time."[10] Other critics, equally willing to see the play as an adaptation of the conventions and techniques of Roman comedy, have expressed less enthusiasm. Florence May Snell, who edited *A Tale of a Tub* in 1915, confessed bafflement: "Jollity, actuality, life," she wrote, "but hopeless confusion which leaves the spectator wondering vaguely what it is all about."[11] Freda L. Townsend agreed, pointing out that Jonson used twice as much complication as he needed and gave his most careful attention to relatively unimportant characters like Hannibal Puppy, Dido Wispe, Pol-Marten, and the other rustics.[12] All three of these critics—Herford, Snell, and Townsend—wanted to judge the play by the norm of Roman comedy; but whereas Herford indicated happiness with the result, the other two did not. The difference between these two reactions to *A Tale of a Tub* is the difference between thinking of the play as a literary document and thinking of it as taking place on the stage. Snell and Townsend tried to do the latter and failed—understandably, for to visualize *A Tale of a Tub* in performance (or for that matter most of Jonson's plays) requires both mental agility and a knowledge of theater that many of us lack. Nevertheless it is important that we try to do just that, for a proper understanding of this play depends upon seeing it in terms of an action somewhat different from the one that the conventions of Roman comedy tempt us to impose upon it.

All good postclassical adaptations of Roman comedy present this same problem to some degree, though in slighter comedies the degree can diminish to the vanishing point. Ancient comedy, whether Greek or Roman, works upon an assumption that we moderns do not entirely share. Aristotle expressed it very well when he wrote that man is by nature a political animal, not a whole in himself but merely part of a state, which is an entity "clearly prior to the family and to the individual."[13] Ancient tragedy was based upon the same assumption and usually took the state as its theater; comedy by contrast stayed at home, but the family affair of comedy usually had political implications. Northrop Frye has written that "New Comedy unfolds from what may be described as a comic Oedipus situation."[14] He might have called it more precisely a domesticated Oedipus situation. The tragedy of Oedipus is not that he replaced his father but that he replaced his king. Take away Laius' kingship and its explicit implications for Thebes as a whole, and all that remains is material for a comedy—an embarrassing family affair, which some Greeks might have regretted and others certainly would have laughed at but few would have thought tragic. English comedy of the Elizabethan variety places the emphasis differently. Compelled by its context of Christian humanism to recognize the importance of any human being, however humble, and to regard families as intrinsically sacred things, it must either completely dehumanize the characters in a classically derived comic pattern and declare the whole business a farce or make some shift to nullify the damage that almost any ancient plot will do to some of the innocuous characters involved. The author of *Ralph Roister Doister*, one may recall, did both things, creating caricatures out of all the characters except

Dame Christian Custance and making full restitution to her in the form of an honest husband at the dénouement. A Roman playwright would not have cared what happened to that lady. Even Shakespeare in writing *The Comedy of Errors*, which is mistakenly treated as pure farce by most critics, rewarded Aegeon and old Aemilia with genuine happiness at the end and promised the personable Luciana a dignified marriage in compensation for the pain he had made her capable of suffering. *A Tale of a Tub* is like both of these in respect to having marriages at the end, but there the resemblance grows cloudy. The marriages in Jonson's play scarcely compensate anyone; in fact, as Miss Townsend has implied, they are largely gratuitous, bestowed on people who in no conventional sense merit them—who in an ordinary comedy would have merited no kind of consideration at all. Jonson's play, therefore, though it differs from classical comedy, differs also from the customary Elizabethan adaptation of classical comedy. It moves toward marriages, but the marriages have no discernible justification. The intrigue, such as it is, is like a papier-mâché monster in a Christmas parade. As children we marvel at it; as adults we recognize that the power that moves it is not its own. Obviously *A Tale of a Tub* is a papier-mâché figure of some kind, and the question that emerges when one takes the play seriously is, "What makes it go?"

A review of the intrigue may suggest the direction in which an answer lies. As the play begins, we have the young son (Squire Tub) of a possessive mother (Lady Tub) making plans to elope with the constable's daughter (Awdrey Turfe). The occasion is St. Valentine's Day, traditionally the time when young people choose their mates. With only this much essential business and no more Jonson might have moved ahead to a satisfactory intrigue comedy, adding at the appropriate stages, of course, his machinator and a rival suitor. Yet he confused the complication by making the machinator a clergyman and the rival suitor a justice of the peace. The result was something that threatened to involve a whole community and become social satire, as in a modest way it did. On inspection the functions of the intrigue actually turn out to be these: the debasement of the gentry (represented by the young man and his mother), the compromising of the local judiciary, the mocking of the officers of the law, and the corruption of the clergy. In no sense can the intrigue be said to lead naturally to the marriages, which alone save the day and make possible the restoration of order. Awdrey Turfe marries neither the simple-minded John Clay, to whom her father's Valentine lottery betrothed her, nor one of her two upper-class suitors, but Pol-Marten, a rehabilitated worker from the salt mines now serving as gentleman usher to Squire Tub's mother. (The other marriage, apparently thrown in for healthy good measure, involves the constable's serving man, Hannibal Puppy, and Lady Tub's maid, Dido Wispe.) If the intrigue really mattered here, as it always matters even in the sentimental adaptations of Roman comedy, the main participants in it should all be out of sorts with one another at the end and hardly ready to make peace and restore order. Yet, except for Clay, who cries into his plate at the dinner, they not only make peace but seem genuinely pleased that things have worked out as they have; and even Clay takes his seat at Medlay's masque at the end, which recapitulates in "motions" the day's activities. Obviously the community has passed its crisis and will survive to meet another Valentine's Day, yet it is doubtful whether anyone on the stage understands why. In-and-In Medlay's motions, designed to provide an official explanation, in reality explain nothing. They are official gestures, like the formal motions or gestures which dignify the superficial and accidental public maneuvers that people go through as preludes to such serious activities as marrying, crowning kings, and burying the dead. What really "happens" in this play is the submerged action; and that action is neither specifically classical nor specifically Christian but antecedent to civilization itself, something seldom visible and perhaps ultimately inexplicable even with the help of modern anthropology and depth psychology, and yet something that must always be acknowledged implicitly, as here, and accepted by everyone concerned.

Jonson's prologue to *A Tale of a Tub* is a serious poem on this theme and advises us of the serious intent of his play. He avoids sentimentality by using broad but well-controlled irony:

No State-affaires, nor any politique *Club,*
    Pretend wee in our *Tale,* here, of a *Tub,*
But acts of *Clownes* and *Constables,* to day
    Stuffe out the *Scenes* of our ridiculous *Play.*
A Coopers wit, or some such busie Sparke,
    Illumining the high *Constable,* and his *Clarke,*
And all the Neighbour-hood, from old Records,
    Of antick Proverbs, drawne from *Whitson-Lord's,*
And their Authorities, at *Wakes* and *Ales,*
    With countrey precedents, and old Wives Tales;
Wee bring you now, to shew what different things
    The *Cotes* of *Clownes,* are from the *Courts* of *Kings.*

It is difficult to see how one could miss the irony of these twelve lines and assume that because Jonson wrote of "clowns and constables" he meant to point up some superficial difference between cottages and courts.[15] Squire Tub, who steps out of the play to read the Epilogue at the end, makes explicit both the general applicability of the play and its gentle rebuke to those who would take it merely as a simple-minded farce:

This Tale of mee, the *Tub* of *Totten-Court*,
  A *Poet*, first invented for your sport.
Wherein the fortune of most empty Tubs
  Rowling in love, are shewne; and with what rubs,
W'are commonly encountered: when the wit
  Of the whole *Hundred* so opposeth it.

(Epilogue, ll. 1-6)

"Most empty tubs" is sweeping enough to include most of those able to see or read a play, and most of those would seem to be lumped together, too, in Tub's explanation of why he got Medlay to provide a masque: "That you be pleas'd, who come to see a *Play*, / With those that heare, and marke not what wee say" (Epilogue, ll. 13–14). The ridiculous version of *A Tale of a Tub* is the version preserved in Medlay's masque, which makes the complaisant rustics who approve it seem no more ridiculous than the seventeenth-century spectators who saw only that much in the play as a whole. To avoid being judged, the modern reader must dissociate himself from all those who heard without marking and pay attention to what the characters talk about when they are not busy moving the plot around.

    Much of the talk in the play serves to establish the claim to status of those who engage in it, and it is this sort of thing which makes the play funny and meaningful rather than the much ado about nothing that keeps everybody hopping. The Tubs have wealth and consequently have been able to buy visible symbols: a pretentious dwelling, servants in livery, and masques on occasion to celebrate with appropriate device the antiquity of their house and family, "Originall from Salt-Peeter" (v.vii.8). Justice Bramble, who laments the inability of people to get his name right (Preamble), rejoices in the status and superior mobility that learning has conferred upon him:

> . . . the incorrigible
> Knot-headed beast, the Clownes, or Constables,
> Still let them graze; eat Sallads; chew the Cud:
> All the Towne-musicke will not move a log.
>
> (I.v.21–24)

Yet the grazing clowns make their claims, too. Constable Tobie Turfe, momentarily forgetting himself and using the term *clown* to refer to slow-moving Clay, proceeds to apply the term to himself and make it virtuous with a questionable etymology:

> A *Midlesex* Clowne; and one of *Finsbury:*
> They were the first Colon's o' the kingdome here:
> The Primitory Colon's; my *D'ogenes* sayes.
>
> (I.iii.34–36)

And Diogenes obliges with a confirmation:

> Sir, Colonus is an Inhabitant:
> A Clowne originall: as you'ld zay a Farmer,
> A Tiller o' th' Earth, ere sin' the *Romans*
> Planted their Colonie first, which was in *Midlesex*.
>
> (I.iii.40–43)

To-Pan the tinker, not to be outdone by Middlesex, presents the case for his native Kent:

> . . . for there they landed
> All Gentlemen, and come in with the Conquerour,
> Mad *Iulius Caesar;* who built *Dover*-Castle:
> My Ancestor *To-Pan*, beat the first Ketle-drum,

Avore 'hun, here vrom *Dover* on the March:
Which peice of monumentall copper hangs
Up, scourd, at *Hammer-smith* yet; for there they came
Over the *Thames*, at a low water marke;
Vore either *London*, I, or *Kingston* Bridge—
I doubt were kursind.

(1.iii.50–59)

Shortly thereafter, when the prospective son-in-law does finally arrive, Turfe addresses him as "Originous Clay: and *Clay
o' Kilborne* too" (1.iv.4), which combination of epithets he
declares preferable to those of any "vine silken Tub." In
short for all these people status means belonging to some order
of things, and they invariably select for their declared mode
of being the order that will be most flattering to them. The
fact that all of it is sheer pretense is the basis of the humor in
the play and the source of all the waste motion that results.
Tub is not genteel, Bramble is not really learned or clever, and
the clowns are really clowns with no lineage at all worth
setting down.

The only order that holds all these people together is the
order that requires the species to perpetuate itself if it would
survive: Awdrey Turfe is ready for marriage, and thereby
hangs this tale of half-a-dozen empty tubs and the rubs with
which they are encountered. The means whereby all can come
together without resorting to civil war and possible self-
extinction is the ancient device of an established institution so
loosely defined as to enable almost everybody to respect it. We
have such a device in the institution of Christmas, which in
our present secular society now embraces Catholic, Protes-
tant, and Jew in one day out of the year devoted to love and
brotherhood. In this play the institution is St. Valentine's, a
day for coming together and doing something that must be

done. Even the sophisticated cleric respects it, though he observes that the weather is unseasonably cold for seeking mates. It is the saintly bishop's day, and nothing more need be said. Neither he nor his parishioners have the faintest notion who St. Valentine was, any more than we have.

Our ignorance is not likely to be remedied. Scholars do not know what, if any, connection there is between the day we call St. Valentine's and the Roman Lupercal, which fell at about the same time of the year. They do not know which St. Valentine is presumably being honored or whether any St. Valentine did any of the things sometimes attributed to him. All one can be certain of is that the custom of choosing mates on the day was considered to be well established among human beings and animals alike by the time that Chaucer wrote his *Parliament of Fowls* and that the custom has been referred to occasionally in literature since that time. The lottery is apparently a common accompaniment of the procedure—understandably so, since lotteries are still the best known device for throwing any decision into the hands of the gods. The people of Finsbury Hundred know enough to hold a lottery, and that is the extent of their knowledge. Clench the farrier has an idea St. Valentine was one of the Seven Deadly Sins: "Hee was a deadly *Zin*, and dwelt at *High-gate*, / As I have heard, but 't was avore my time" (1.ii.8–9). Diogenes Scriben, the local writer, thinks perhaps the name has been corrupted from "Sim Valentine," because he has never yet found the name "Sin" in any of the parish records. To-Pan thinks he was an innkeeper, and Constable Turfe has the name twisted in his mind to "Son Valentine," which version he bestows beamingly on John Clay. Lady Tub, like Canon Hugh, knows that the saint was supposed to have been a cleric, but she seems to have him confused with some puritanical version of St. Nicholas:

EPILOGUE

> . . . Bishop *Valentine*
> Left us example to doe deeds of Charity
> To feed the hungry; cloath the naked; visit
> The weake, and sicke; to entertaine the poore;
> And give the dead a Christian Funerall;
> These were the workes of piety he did practise,
> And bad us imitate; not looke for Lovers,
> Or handsome Images to please our senses.

(1.vii.8–15)

But Lady Tub knows what all the rest know—that blood stirs at the bottom of the year and must be dealt with one way or another, officially or unofficially. The underlying action of the play is just that: a group of people perpetuating itself by letting the blood have its way. It is very much like what happens in Herrick's *Corinna*, where parents deliberately sleep late and priests take up their station to meet the young people as they come out of the woods. Our interest in the play derives from the fact that the civilization of the group, such as it is, keeps getting in the way. In unconscious presumption they try to control the natural action in a variety of moral and legal ways. Our relief and satisfaction come when the civilization preserves itself in the only way civilization ever can: by relaxing at the crucial moment and letting nature take her course.

The conflict in *A Tale of a Tub* may be said to develop in the following way. On St. Valentine's Eve, with an Awdrey to be married off, Constable Turfe and the others hold a lottery in advance of the holiday and proceed immediately to make arrangements to wed the young woman to John Clay on the following morning. The day is thus acknowledged but not respected, and their violation of its prerogatives opens the door wide for the anarchy which follows. Canon Hugh, caring only for fun and profit, proceeds to make capital of Tub and Bramble, who seek in their turn to subvert the action of the townspeople and capture Awdrey for themselves. Lady Tub sets out in pursuit, ostensibly to rescue her son but actually to profane the day still further by using it as an occasion for sport. At this level of the play we have, point for point, a recognizable version of the Roman comedy plot, in which old ones are gulled and young ones seek their mates; yet the Roman comedy plot comes to precisely nothing. In all Finsbury Hundred the only people not involved in a blasphemous subversion of the day's proper business are Awdrey, who apparently has not been consulted very much, and the serving people, Hannibal Puppy, Dido Wispe, and Pol-Marten. As the day wears on, all the civilized forces cancel themselves out. Turfe, who might well have succeeded in marrying his daughter to John Clay, keeps quibbling over incidental expenses until he loses the initiative to Tub and Bramble; and Tub and Bramble keep getting in one another's way until Lady Tub arrives to add more complications. Eventually control passes by default to the people who by nature ought to have it; and Awdrey, Pol-Marten, Puppy, and Dido slip away in disguise to "take their makes" in the presence of Canon Hugh. It is an outcome to gladden the heart of the ancient saint, wherever and whatever he may be; and the thing that makes it comic is the acceptance it receives from winners and losers alike.

There are several ways one might generalize about this play. One could say that it presents the triumph of St. Valentine. One could also say that it presents the victory of man's genuine impulses over the shaky institutions that man has devised for the purpose of organizing his impulses: that is, the victory of nature over society. But one could, and should, note that it presents the proper relationship between nature and art; for art in this play, prematurely invoked, restricts and all but destroys the social institutions it is committed to preserve and perpetuate. The proper place for art, though admittedly art is represented poorly in these proceedings, is indicated by Medlay's feeble masque at the end, which presides over Nature's fait accompli, marking man's acceptance and re-creation of something God has wrought instead of man's arrogation of the right to work entirely in God's stead. This was Jonson's own use of art, as an activity that began and ended in respect for the nature of things. As satirist he could deplore man's wilful or foolish perversions of that nature; but respect for nature itself required him increasingly to represent men, not monsters, and to keep his data accurate. From *Poetaster* through *Bartholomew Fair*, at least, he presents on his stage no improbable fictions but things as they are, or as they might be in the course of nature itself, given the proper situation and circumstances.

A Tale of a Tub celebrates the kind of miracle that Jonson the playwright readily recognized: that is, the kind of miracle represented by such day-to-day metamorphoses as the exhaustion or purgation of a humor, marriage, and the reconciliation of friends—all means whereby the natural world perennially renews itself. In *Every Man in His Humor* he gave only perfunctory notice, it is true, to the marriage of Edward and Bridget; but he celebrated fully there that change in their elders from selfish fear to generosity which insured the continuing happiness of the two young people. Then for a time Jonson let natural changes like these all but disappear from his plays as he moved ahead to experimentation with comical satire, in which the satirist was expected to impose correction, and after that to the even darker comedies *Volpone* and *Epicene*. In *The Alchemist*, however, beneath a vast heap of dead and untransmutable matter he discovered once more for his viewers a hope of renewal—discovered it not so much in the betrothal of Dame Pliant to Lovewit as in the reestablishment of loyalty and affection between master and servant. Finally in *Bartholomew Fair*, although that play too had as its ostensible objective the mating of the young, Jonson presented a general transmutation of principals, most of whom by coming to the fair found themselves changed for the better, turned from supercilious observers of the human comedy surrounding them into willing participants in it, "flesh and blood." *A Tale of a Tub* is, of course, a much slighter work; but it treats of the same humanity, and it presents a similar texture of details concretely and credibly rendered. Moreover the marriage of Awdrey to Pol-Marten, which provides a focus for the plot, is really only one part of a larger springtime renewal that comes to the entire community of Finsbury Hundred. And here, as in *Bartholomew Fair*, Jonson seems to have penetrated to the mysterious mainsprings of collective human experience and so made his skillful New Comedy play not merely diverting but perennially reassuring to those who watch or read.

In short, *A Tale of a Tub* begins and, like *Bartholomew Fair*, ends in acceptance of the human situation. Society falters in *A Tale of a Tub* and provides a day's excitement; but society in Finsbury Hundred lives close to nature and stumbles only to be revived, like Antaeus, by contact with the earth. One imagines that even Downright and Surly in a place like Finsbury Hundred would have been likely to change, just as Quarlous was changed by his contact with the fair. There is nothing quite like that in Jonson's earliest plays or in those that we definitely know to have been among his latest. One feels that he was most likely to have written *A Tale of a Tub* in the decade that saw compilation of his great Folio of 1616, but certainty about that matter is impossible. The play most like it is Shakespeare's *The Merry Wives of Windsor*, which is an anomaly at the midpoint of another distinguished career and has also often puzzled the critics. Yet in the rustic world of such plays as these metamorphosis is a daily phenomenon, and renewal is within the expectation of many of the creatures that live there, among them the poor in spirit and disaffected critics of men and manners.

Looking back over the whole span of Jonson's dramatic work for the public theaters, one immediately recognizes that rustic nature appears but rarely there. Jonson's subject was usually city life—indeed contemporary London life, though the place could sometimes be Rome or Venice and the age could vary. The naturalistic detail of a play like *A Tale of a Tub*, however, is consonant with a fairly large complex of manifestations distributed among the poems and masques and involving almost all of his plays, and this suggests a Jonson who included in his idea of nature all the given conditions of the world about him and as artist treated them with equal respect, whether urban or rustic, past or present. As we have already noted, Alvin Kernan, in ruling out of Jonson's thinking any strong impulse to see in nature the beneficent, supernatural force that Shakespeare sometimes saw operating there, points to Jonson's strong belief in a nature of physical law which, when occasionally askew, would tend to come right again because of "a defect inherent in vice and folly which leads them to overreach themselves."[16] This is certainly a legitimate way of looking at the matter, but at least one thing more needs to be said. Jonson was always enough of a Catholic to believe that the world had been created good and, even though now an imperfect, fallen world, would remain essentially good throughout the rest of time. Such a conviction was enough to justify for him his self-appointed role of benevolent satirist, but it also tempered his satire and kept it from becoming genuinely bitter for more than brief periods. Normally he scourged his apes—Sir Politic and Lady Would-Be, Mammon,

Morose, and Busy, to mention only a few—in love, with tolerance for their weaknesses, and with the possibility of their redemption always in view. That some (e.g., Volpone and Mosca) could not or would not improve, he recognized; but for him the miracle inherent in the natural world was that most of her foolish and wicked creatures might with the proper stimulus (and occasionally with no apparent stimulus at all) change for the better. In the sense that this world continually moved both to punish the incorrigibly overreaching wicked and to provide stimuli for the rest to undergo a moral metamorphosis, even in the midst of their mischief, it presented a "supernatural" aspect even while it was moving steadily along in unruffled obedience to mechanical laws.

At the outset of his career, however, Jonson probably had not thought very deeply either about the world or about his role as poet in it; and, as we have seen, he was able to allow the young hero of *Every Man in His Humor* to declaim about the divinity of poetry and declare its separateness from the world of people and things. Three years later in *Poetaster* he was condemning the same stance, and five years after that he was prepared to proclaim (in the published version of *Volpone*) his responsibility as a poet to be involved in the world, interpret it, and effect its improvement. Because Jonson suppressed his earliest plays, we cannot be sure just when he began to particularize his scene with realistic detail; but we have the evidence of *Every Man out of His Humor* to show that he had at least begun the practice by 1599, and with his participation in the composition of *Eastward Ho!* in 1605 he identified himself publicly with the mode of city comedy. Thereafter Jonson's dramatic poetry was manifestly a poetry in and of the tangible world.

Also as early as *Every Man in His Humor* Jonson came to the conviction, best stated in the biblical "Judge not that ye be not judged," that no human being committed to the correction of other human beings can avoid indefinitely the pitfalls of human self-interest and pride. As kings are kings only by grace and judges are judges *under* the law, so moral and satiric poets must proceed under the sanction of some higher authority if their activity is to avoid being self-centered or personally vindictive. In moving to this position Jonson was relying on nothing more esoteric than the principal of hierarchy, which in his England and in any other genuinely Christian community of the time was expected not only to give order to the human establishment but to preserve all ranks in that order from the ravages of self-interest. It was thus understandable that, once set on the course of exploring the relation of poet or any creative artist to society, he should come in time to consider what happens when the human hierarchy itself begins to falter. The first two great comedies of his maturity provide at least negative answers to an inquiry into this matter. First, *Volpone* shows us what happens when a creative genius serving no one but himself misses his one opportunity to escape the trap of self and attempts to violate a potential savior; society, failing though not entirely dead, makes a show of order in condemning his perverted creativity but continues steadily on its own downward course. *Epicene* presents a similar but less pernicious figure, who attempts to maneuver in a social order that has already disintegrated; his fate, as we saw, is simply to spin wildly out of control and end in absurdity.

Yet *Epicene* does move us forward to the final step in the exploration in that it begins to uncover the capacity of fallen human nature to right itself. This we see fleetingly at the end of the play when Dauphine reveals his successful plot to triumph over his uncle and insure some kind of succession in spite of corruption and decay. Morose's wickedness, of course, does not make Dauphine right any more than the triumph of Face and Lovewit in Jonson's next play, *The Alchemist,* means that these partners in petty crime do not richly deserve the punishment they never get. The principle involved here is the Christian paradox that was as fundamental to Jonson as it was ancient and had been given a recent apt statement in Shakespeare: "Some falls are means the happier to arise" (*Cymbeline,* IV.ii.403). *Some* falls, one must insist—not all. The paradox of the Fortunate Fall does not rule out damnation, and it is fortunate only when the Creator elects to make it so. This, as we saw in an earlier chapter, is analogous to the idea of justice presented in the Parable of the Lord of the Vineyard (Matt. 20:1-16); it is also consonant with the "unreasonable" ethic presented in the Book of Job. No visible good whatever is generated by Volpone's fall; and only the faint possibility of good is visible at the end of *Epicene*. Yet out of the rubble of a fallen society, which is where *The Alchemist* begins, comes the clear symbol of order—a master and mistress presiding over a reconstituted establishment, made possible by the creativity and genius of a faithful servant. In *Bartholomew Fair,* Jonson's orderly symbol of human riot and disorder, the paradox is even more apparent; and the dust and smell of flesh themselves become the means whereby pride can be humbled and communion in a faltering society reestablished.

And all these demonstrations, we have suggested in this study, were for Jonson himself explorations. As the most learned poet in his time, perhaps the most prideful, and certainly the most ambitious to serve as a public voice, he needed to know the liabilities inherent in his talents and his aspirations. There were no clear precedents to instruct him, and he could learn experientially only by creating in his own art the conditions of social disaster and contemplating the consequences for poets, machinators, makers, and would-be critics of men and manners. In part he learned what to avoid, but he also found confirmation for an inherited and ancient antidote to despair. If there was ever a strain of sentimental optimism in Jonson, he suppressed it; but he suppressed as well whatever tendencies he may have had toward the sentimental pessimism with which some current criticism confidently saddles him. What he did maintain throughout his career was a hardheaded, orthodox belief in the fundamental goodness of creation. Without that belief he might have deplored the world, but he could never have begun to consider it corrigible; and the belief usually manifested itself in one way or another in all but his most somber work. *A Tale of a Tub* presents it without embarrassment. As the last play to be performed during Jonson's lifetime, its presence in the author's favor strengthens our view that an abiding faith in goodness continued to brighten his life even in those years when an accumulation of personal disappointments, old age, and a time out of joint might have led a lesser man to give up hope entirely.

Notes

NOTES TO CHAPTER ONE

1. See Larry S. Champion, *Ben Jonson's "Dotages": A Reconsideration of the Late Plays* (Lexington: University Press of Kentucky, 1967).

2. Jonas A. Barish, *Ben Jonson and the Language of Prose Comedy* (Cambridge, Mass.: Harvard University Press, 1960).

3. Edward B. Partridge, *The Broken Compass: A Study of the Major Comedies of Ben Jonson* (New York: Columbia University Press, 1958), pp. 234, 236.

4. Gabriele Bernhard Jackson, *Vision and Judgment in Jonson's Drama* (New Haven: Yale University Press, 1968), p. 166.

5. Ibid., p. 169.

6. Robert Ornstein, "Shakespearian and Jonsonian Comedy," *Shakespeare Survey* 22 (1969): 46.

7. Students of Jonson are indebted to Coburn Gum's detailed study, *The Aristophanic Comedies of Ben Jonson* (The Hague: Mouton, 1969), which also has a great deal to say about Jonson's use of Latin comedy; Gum's bibliography is especially valuable. Another study that contains commentary on these matters is G. C. Thayer's *Ben Jonson: Studies in the Plays* (Norman: University of Oklahoma Press, 1963).

8. All quotations from Jonson's work are from *Ben Jonson*, ed. Charles H. Herford and Percy and Evelyn Simpson, 11 vols. (Oxford: Clarendon Press, 1925–1952). Further citations in these notes will appear as "Herford and Simpson."

9. Thayer argues that the presentation of humors in *Every Man in His Humor* is "a display of the relatively pleasant foibles which contribute to the comic way of the world" and that generally by *humors* Jonson means

manners (*Ben Jonson*, pp. 20–21). Jonson was well aware of the confusion of these terms, of course, but the humors of a Kitely or of the elder Knowell in *Every Man in His Humor* are surely more than manners; see the present author's "Jonson's Revisions of *Every Man in His Humor*," *Studies in Philology* 59 (1962): 641–650.

10. Robert C. Jones, "The Satirist's Retirement in Jonson's 'Apologetical Dialogue,' " *ELH* 34 (1967): 447–467.

11. Jonson is usually said to have derived his statement from Strabo, *Geography*, 1.ii.5; see Herford and Simpson, 1:683. Jonson, however, was undoubtedly familiar also with Quintilian's words to the same effect, *Institutio Oratoria*, 1. Preface. 9–10, trans. H. E. Butler (London: W. Heinemann, 1921), pp. 8–11.

12. Alvin Kernan, *The Cankered Muse: Satire of the English Renaissance* (New Haven: Yale University Press, 1959), pp. 156–164.

13. The corresponding passage in the Folio is at iv.ii.115–122. The Folio, of course, omits references to deity.

14. Finding traces of the early satiric expositor in Jonson's mature work is fairly common, and a number of writers have noted them in passing. Barish, for example, relates him to Brainworm and young Knowell of Folio *Every Man in His Humor*, Peregrine, Truewit, Quarlous, Winwife, and Waspe (*Ben Jonson*, pp. 137–141, 143, 147, 194, 215). See also Kernan, *The Cankered Muse*, p. 164. Barish (p. 177) even hints at a progressive development. Harry Levin has related Surly of *The Alchemist* to Asper and to all the others who stand for the "sterner Jonson"; see his article *"The Tempest* and *The Alchemist,"* *Shakespeare Survey* 22 (1969): 54. No one, however, has dealt at length with the matter, shown how the expositor merges with other types that Jonson uses (notably the machinator), or demonstrated how Jonson's changing disposition of the expositor reflects his changing attitude toward the role of the comic poet.

NOTES TO CHAPTER TWO

1. Northrop Frye finds the conventions of New Comedy evident in *Every Man out of His Humor* but thinks that Jonson was referring to the sardonic tone when he spoke of it as closer to Old Comedy, "Old and New Comedy," *Shakespeare Survey* 22 (1969): 3.

2. Robert E. Knoll, *Ben Jonson's Plays: An Introduction* (Lincoln: University of Nebraska Press, 1964), p. 47.

3. For example, John J. Enck has called it "scarcely a play," *Jonson and the Comic Truth* (Madison: University of Wisconsin Press, 1957), p. 56.

4. O. J. Campbell has shown that Jonson in these plays was seeking to adapt formal satire to the dramatic form, *Comicall Satyre and Shakespeare's "Troilus and Cressida"* (San Marino, Calif.: Huntington Library, 1938), pp. 54–134. See also Alvin Kernan's suggestion that here Jonson was trying with only partial success to manage the figure of the satirist within the action of a play (*The Cankered Muse*, pp. 156–164).

5. On this and succeeding events in the "War of the Theaters" see Alfred Harbage, *Shakespeare and the Rival Traditions* (New York: Macmillan, 1952), pp. 90–119.

6. *The Triple Thinkers: Twelve Essays on Literary Subjects*, rev. ed. (New York: Oxford University Press, 1948), pp. 213–232.

7. See Herford and Simpson, 3:602–603, Appendix x, "The Original Conclusion in the Quartos."

8. Ibid.

9. Ibid., 3:599.

10. Brinsley Nicholson and C. H. Herford, eds., *Ben Jonson* (London: T. Fisher Unwin, n.d.), 1:113.

11. Enck seems to suspect that something significant lies behind Jonson's doubling of these characters, but he concludes that it was mainly a device to hold the loose structure of the play together (*Jonson and the Comic Truth*, p. 57).

12. Thayer observes that Cordatus, in addition to explaining the action and the author's comic theory, "also represents a side of Jonson's public personality" (*Ben Jonson*, p. 30).

13. Ernest William Talbert has demonstrated convincingly how the Renaissance moral interpretation of mythology lies behind Jonson's use of the myths of Echo and Narcissus, Niobe, and Actaeon and helps to give coherence to the play, "The Classical Mythology and the Structure of *Cynthia's Revels*," *Philological Quarterly* 22 (1943): 193–210.

14. Jackson considers poetry the principal concern of *Poetaster*, but she sees the problem as deriving from a choice of subject matter; that is, Ovid celebrates material things and Virgil, spiritual things (*Vision and Judgment in Ben Jonson's Drama*, pp. 20–30).

15. See this study, chap. 1, pp. 8–10.

16. See *The Complete Works of Sir Philip Sidney*, ed. Albert Feuillerat (Cambridge: Cambridge University Press, 1923), 3:32–35.

17. This is partly the position taken by O. J. Campbell, who calls Ovid's story "the essential plot of *Poetaster*" (*Comicall Satyre*, p. 128; see also pp. 112ff.). Eugene Waith similarly finds morality Ovid's conspicuous lack and considers morality the sine qua non for Jonson's true poet; he, however, regards Horace as central to the play ("The Poet's Morals in Jonson's *Poetaster*," *Modern Language Quarterly* 12, 1951: 13–19).

18. Cf. the apt statement by Jackson: "From *Poetaster* onward all imagination used for personal gratification becomes sinister, a force which undermines society" (*Vision and Judgment*, p. 30). Appropriately she cites the creativity of Subtle, Mosca, and Catiline as examples of the undesirable use of ingenuity.

19. See his description of the activity of a poet in *Discoveries*, ed. Herford and Simpson, 8:636.

NOTES TO CHAPTER THREE

1. The title page of the Quarto bears the date 1607; but the date of February 11, 1607, following Jonson's Epistle Dedicatory indicates that the volume probably came out in February or March of 1608 by the modern way of reckoning.

2. See Mario Praz, "Ben Jonson's Italy," in *The Flaming Heart* (Garden City, N.Y.: Doubleday, 1958), pp. 168–185.

3. See chap. 1, pp. 13–14.

4. This point has been argued ably by Ralph Nash, "The Comic Intent of *Volpone*," *Studies in Philology* 44 (1947): 26–40.

5. For example, Northrop Frye calls *Volpone* "exceptional in being a kind of comic imitation of a tragedy, with the point of Volpone's hybris carefully marked" (*Anatomy of Criticism*, Princeton: Princeton University Press, 1957, p. 165). See the useful examination of this matter by P. H. Davison, "*Volpone* and the Old Comedy," *Modern Language Quarterly* 24 (1963): 151–157.

6. See the illuminating comments on *Sejanus* and *Volpone* in Alan C. Dessen's *Jonson's Moral Comedy* (Evanston, Ill.: Northwestern University Press, 1971), pp. 70–75; see also the present author's "The Nature of the Conflict in Jonson's *Sejanus*," *Vanderbilt Studies in the Humanities*, vol. 1, ed. R. C. Beatty, J. P. Hyatt, and M. K. Spears (Nashville: Vanderbilt University Press, 1951), pp. 217–219.

7. *Ben Jonson's Plays*, pp. 83–93.

8. See Herford and Simpson, 11:514.

9. Knoll, *Ben Jonson's Plays*, p. 81.

10. By Stefan Zweig and Jules Romains, performed in Paris in 1928 and, in an English translation by Ruth Langner, in New York that same year. This version has had numerous revivals.

11. *The Broken Compass*, pp. 70–113.

12. "The Double Plot in *Volpone*," *Modern Philology* 51 (1953): 83–92.

13. Ibid., p. 84.

14. Ibid.

15. K. M. Burton makes this point with respect to *Sejanus*, suggesting that the citizens of Rome are responsible for the tragic dilemma in which they find themselves; see her article "The Political Tragedies of Chapman and Ben Jonson," *Essays in Criticism* 2 (1952): 404.

16. Alvin Kernan has a good discussion of the penchant of Volpone and Mosca for acting; see his edition, *Ben Jonson: "Volpone"* (New Haven: Yale University Press, 1962), pp. 6–26.

17. Thomas M. Greene writes, "The subject of *Volpone* is Protean man, man without core and principle and substance. It is an anatomy of metamorphosis, the exaltations and nightmares of our psychic discontinuities" ("Ben Jonson and the Centered Self," *Studies in English Literature* 10, 1970: 325–348).

18. Thayer has an interesting discussion of Volpone as poet manqué, in which he presents Volpone as a "Dionysian and thus seriously at odds with the pervasive spirit of Apollo" (*Ben Jonson*, pp. 60–64). To regard Volpone in this way, however, as "the deficient rather than the ideal poet," leaves us in the ethical dilemma posed first by Brainworm's performance in *Every Man in His Humor* and later by Face's in *The Alchemist*, both of which are pardoned in the end. There is really only one kind of poet in Jonson. In his view, the human poet, insofar as he is a poet, is Apollonian, but he must always be subject to some superior authority. Any poet, in short, who knows no master or patron is a poet manqué.

19. For comment on Lady Would-Be's parrotlike qualities see Helena Watts Baum, *The Satiric and the Didactic in Jonson's Comedy* (Chapel Hill: University of North Carolina Press, 1947), p. 174.

20. See Partridge, *The Broken Compass*, pp. 72–77, and also the more recent study by Charles H. Hallett, "The Satanic Nature of Volpone," *Philological Quarterly* 49 (1970): 41–55.

21. For example, Harry Levin has called *Volpone* Jonson's "last experiment in poetic justice"; see his "Jonson's Metempsychosis," *Philological Quarterly* 22 (1943): 238. Thayer (*Ben Jonson*, p. 64) finds the play ethi-

cally satisfying because Volpone's action, he thinks, was fundamentally avaricious and thus deserving of the punishment it brought. Dessen finds the morality element especially strong in *Volpone;* see his summarizing statement (*Jonson's Moral Comedy*, p. 103).

22. Levin, "Jonson's Metempsychosis," p. 234.

23. Barish, *Ben Jonson*, p. 143.

24. Critics differ sharply about Celia. Thayer, for example, calls her an "idiot" and says that her virtue is a "mere parody of virtue" (*Ben Jonson*, p. 52). Dessen (*Jonson's Moral Comedy*, pp. 88–90) cites others who take this position but argues against it. See also the arguments of Charles A. Hallett in "Jonson's Celia: A Reinterpretation of *Volpone*," *Studies in Philology* 58 (1971): 50–61, 68; and "The Satanic Nature of Volpone," *Philological Quarterly* 49 (1970): 41–55.

25. *Every Man in His Humor* (1616), v.iii.112–114; see also the Quarto version, v.iii.210–214.

26. Judd Arnold seems to take this literally, suggesting that since Celia is already married, concern about her chastity is exaggerated. See "The Double Plot in *Volpone*. A Note on Jonsonian Dramatic Structure," *Seventeenth-Century News* 23 (1965): 50.

27. See John S. Weld's "Christian Comedy: *Volpone*," *Studies in Philology* 51 (1954): 172–193, especially his comments about folly, p. 173.

28. See the account in L. C. Knights's *Drama and Society in the Age of Jonson* (New York: Barnes and Noble, n.d.), pp. 200–206. Knights's important study first appeared in 1937.

29. See comments by T. S. Eliot, "Ben Jonson," in *Selected Essays, 1917–1932* (New York: Harcourt, Brace, 1932), pp. 137–138.

NOTES TO CHAPTER FOUR

1. "Jonson's Metempsychosis," pp. 238–239.

2. Thayer (*Ben Jonson*, p. 53) regards the magistrates as "extremely dull witted" figures, who pass sentences out of all proportion to the "pleasant crimes" committed. But note the responses of the magistrates in Act v, scene xii, especially the comments of the fourth one.

3. Levin, "Jonson's Metempsychosis," p. 239.

4. Epistle Dedicatory to *Volpone*, ll. 47–70, Herford and Simpson, 3:18–19.

5. Samuel Johnson, *The History of Rasselas, Prince of Abissinia*, ed. R. W. Chapman (Oxford: Clarendon Press, 1927), p. 50.

6. For a discussion of the critical principle involved, see the present author's "The Significance of Ben Jonson's First Requirement for Tragedy: Truth of Argument," *Studies in Philology* 49 (1952): 195–213.

7. *Essays of John Dryden*, ed. W. P. Ker (Oxford: Clarendon Press, 1926), 1:83; Herford and Simpson, 11:516.

8. See the useful comment on this point by L. A. Beaurline, "Ben Jonson and the Illusion of Completeness," *PMLA* 84 (1969): 59.

9. Ray L. Heffner, "Unifying Symbols in the Comedy of Ben Jonson," in *English Stage Comedy: English Institute Essays*, 1954, ed. W. K. Wimsatt, Jr. (New York: Columbia University Press, 1955), pp. 74–97.

10. Partridge, *The Broken Compass*, p. 162.

11. Barish, *Ben Jonson and the Language of Prose Comedy*, pp. 149–185 passim.

12. Herford and Simpson, 10:14ff.

13. Jonson so designates him in the dramatis personae.

14. The views of Northrop Frye are helpful in any consideration of the "darkening" of Jonsonian comedy at this point. Although *Epicene* clearly has the structure of New Comedy and also makes conspicuous use of the "senex or blocking figure" that Frye has identified with the neoclassical form of New Comedy, it has beneath its surface the *agon* of Old Comedy and its conclusion is sardonic, to say the least; see Frye's comments in "Old and New Comedy," pp. 1–4, and *Anatomy of Criticism*, pp. 164–168.

15. *The Complete Works of Samuel Taylor Coleridge*, ed. W. G. T. Shedd (New Haven: Yale University Press, 1954), 6:426.

16. *Ben Jonson's Plays*, pp. 118–121.

17. "Ben Jonson and the Illusion of Completeness," p. 53.

18. Bryant, "Jonson's Revision of *Every Man in His Humor*," pp. 641–650.

19. Brian Gibbons has noted that Surly's role is essentially that of the satirist-presenter at this point, *Jacobean City Comedy* (Cambridge, Mass.: Harvard University Press, 1968), p. 174.

20. *Studies in Jonson's Comedy* (New York: Lamson, Wolffe, 1898), p. 29.

21. *Ben Jonson, l'homme et l'oeuvre* (Paris: Hachette, 1907), p. 357.

22. Partridge, *The Broken Compass*, p. 152.

23. Dessen, *Jonson's Moral Comedy*, pp. 132–134. Dessen cites Jackson (*Vision and Judgment in Jonson's Drama*, pp. 67–69, 90–92) in support of his view.

24. *The Cankered Muse*, pp. 190–191.

25. C. F. Tucker Brooke, "The Renaissance," in *A Literary History of England*, ed. A. C. Baugh (New York: Appleton-Century-Crofts, 1948), p. 563.

26. J. B. Steane, ed., *The Alchemist* (Cambridge: Cambridge University Press, 1967), p. 22.

27. Ibid., p. 90, n. 1.

28. *"The Tempest* and *The Alchemist,"* pp. 47–58.

29. Knoll also has noted (*Ben Jonson's Plays,* p. 134) that *The Alchemist* is a "reworking of the Parable of the Talents," but he suggests that Jonson is here giving a Puritan reading of the Bible (the making of money is evidence of divine favor) to show its shabbiness.

30. See Matt. 25:24–27. This parable with its reference to usury has troubled believers over the years; see also the parable of the lord of the vineyard with its cavalier treatment of "poetic justice," Matt. 20:1–16.

31. F. H. Mares in a recent introduction to the play has suggested that we profit by seeing our own follies here depicted; but he adds, "We are not obliged to make this recognition public," *The Alchemist* (Cambridge, Mass.: Harvard University Press, 1967), p. lviii.

NOTES TO CHAPTER FIVE

1. See Herford and Simpson, 11:13–15.

2. *Jonson's Moral Comedy,* p. 148. The views Dessen cites may be found in E. A. Horsman, ed., *Bartholomew Fair* (London: Methuen, 1960), p. xiii; M. C. Bradbrook, *The Growth and Structure of Elizabethan Comedy* (Berkeley: University of California Press, 1956), p. 146; and Barish, *Ben Jonson and the Language of Prose Comedy,* pp. 222, 225.

3. Dessen, *Jonson's Moral Comedy,* pp. 217–218.

4. Jackson I. Cope, *"Bartholomew Fair* as Blasphemy," *Renaissance Drama,* vol. 8 (Evanston, Ill.: Northwestern University Press, 1965), pp. 127–152.

5. Joel H. Kaplan, "Dramatic and Moral Energy in Ben Jonson's *Bartholomew Fair," Renaissance Drama,* n.s., vol. 3 (Evanston, Ill.: Northwestern University Press, 1970), pp. 137–156.

6. *Jonson and the Comic Truth,* p. 191; Herford and Simpson, 2:137. See also Gibbons, *Jacobean City Comedy,* pp. 179–180.

7. *Ben Jonson's Plays,* p. 148.

8. "Unifying Symbols in the Comedy of Ben Jonson," p. 95.

9. Freda L. Townsend, *Apologie for Bartholomew Fayre* (New York: Modern Language Association of America, 1947), p. 73.

10. James Robinson, "*Bartholomew Fair:* Comedy of Vapors," *Studies in English Literature* 1 (1961): 65–80.

11. Richard Levin, "The Structure of *Bartholomew Fair*," *PMLA* 80 (1965): 172–179.

12. Madeleine Doran says that things of this kind are "simply part of the data which the intriguer manipulates," *Endeavors of Art: A Study of Form in Elizabethan Drama* (Madison: University of Wisconsin Press, 1954), p. 329. Whatever interpretation one gives, the effect is the same.

13. Jonson's half-contemptuous allusions in this passage to Shakespeare's use of fantasy in *The Tempest* have been commented on frequently.

14. Gibbons calls Overdo a parody of the presenter-judge of the comical satires and the morality tradition (*Jacobean City Comedy*, p. 179).

15. Of Ursula, Thayer writes (*Ben Jonson*, p. 133): "She seems to be earth itself, the great Mother, Demeter, and Eve, a great goddess with all her shapes combined in one vast unshape—Ursa Major, the great bear which is also a wagon, appropriate enough to her figure as a bawd." Cope ("*Bartholomew Fair* as Blasphemy," pp. 143–146) sees her as "the very champion of discord, of the lust, theft, fighting, and litigation which dominate a legalistic world gone berserk" and identifies her as "*Ate, Discordia* herself." One of the most useful comments on Ursula is that by Eugene M. Waith in his introduction to the play: "No comedy of Jonson's—perhaps none of any author's—exudes more of the 'life force' which Bernard Shaw so admired, Old Ursula, sweating profusely in her pig-booth, 'all fire and fat,' is the perfect emblem of this force, but there is hardly a character who does not share in it" (*Ben Jonson: Bartholomew Fair*, New Haven: Yale University Press, 1963, p. 4). Obviously Ursula is symbolically complex in that like any other bawd she combines flesh, generation, and disorder in a single figure; she literally represents the ground, good and bad, of our being as human creatures. The beauty of Jonson's characterization here is that he does not sentimentalize it but rather lets the disturbing ambiguity remain. Falstaff is Shakespeare's parallel, and even greater, creation.

16. In recent years the role of Quarlous has at last begun to receive appropriate attention. For example, Richard Levin ("The Structure of *Bartholomew Fair*," pp. 175–176, 177) comments on Quarlous's choric function throughout the play, but he sees him as sharing that function with Winwife. Cope ("*Bartholomew Fair* as Blasphemy," pp. 151–152) see Quarlous as a reactionary: by marrying the widow at the end he has "inherited hell . . . continued and intensified the old errors in a new way by embracing sterility

as if it were to be possessed." Dessen's study (*Jonson's Moral Comedy*, pp. 216–217 and passim) gives us a similarly unregenerate Quarlous; the young man begins with limited insights into the corruption of his times but surrenders even these when he joins the "sport" of the Fair and opportunistically marries Dame Purecraft for her money.

17. Attention was focused on Troubleall first by Heffner ("Unifying Symbols," pp. 90–91), who found in the madman a symbol of the universal "human craving for clearly defined authority" and the primary unifying device of the play. Dessen, who sees the structure of *Bartholomew Fair* somewhat differently, regards Troubleall more as a foil to Overdo (*Jonson's Moral Comedy*, p. 187).

18. Cope calls him "the specter of an ambiguously conceived destiny" ("*Bartholomew Fair* as Blasphemy," p. 140) and suggests that he is a blind destiny, made so by an omnipotent but equally blind "God," Justice Overdo. The distinction between calling Troubleall a destiny and calling him an agent of destiny, however, is a crucial one. Agents of destiny have traditionally been blind (e.g., Tiresias) or mad (e.g., Cassandra); Quarlous's term for Troubleall, "ragged prophet," is accurate. The fact that Jonson does not objectify his metaphysical background cannot be taken as conclusive proof that such a background is being discredited. In a play like *Bartholomew Fair* honesty requires that such things be left mysterious. Even a semifacetious dramatization (e.g., the dream-vision of Jupiter in *Cymbeline*) would have been quite out of place here.

19. Levin ("The Structure of *Bartholomew Fair*," p. 178) recognizes the fortuity of these proceedings and puts it down to "Lucke and Saint Bartholomew."

20. Barish speaks of the fair sympathetically throughout. He acknowledges the "dangers" that inhabit there, but he sees it as having a salutary function: "The play views the excesses of the season unsentimentally, but indulgently, as a product of irredeemable human weakness, and one chief office of the Fair is to lure or coerce back into the human fold the numerous kill-joys who threaten it" (*Ben Jonson and the Language of Prose Comedy*, p. 222). By contrast Levin ("The Structure of *Bartholomew Fair*," p. 179) considers the fair as a "sordid, though certainly lusty" background for the action that takes place there. Dessen (*Jonson's Moral Comedy*, pp. 148–149) seems to agree.

21. *Twelfth Night*, v.i.386.

22. *Othello*, v.ii.304.

23. *The Tempest*, v.i.275–276.

24. See the similar comment on this point by E. A. Horsman, in his edition of *Bartholomew Fair*, p. xxviii.

NOTES TO CHAPTER SIX

1. Printed but never actually published; see Herford and Simpson, 9:85–86.

2. Ibid., 11:515.

3. Ibid.

4. *Ben Jonson's "Dotages,"* p. 133.

5. This is partly Champion's position. See also Partridge, *The Broken Compass*, p. 185, and Knoll, *Ben Jonson's Plays*, p. 165.

6. Champion (*Ben Jonson's "Dotages,"* pp. 134–135) considers even this a piece of satire.

7. Herford and Simpson, 11:163–164.

8. Ibid., 11:166.

9. Knoll, *Ben Jonson's Plays*, pp. 18–20.

10. Herford and Simpson, 1:291.

11. Florence May Snell, ed. *A Tale of a Tub* (London: Longmans, Green, 1915), p. xxxiii.

12. *Apologie for Bartholomew Fayre*, pp. 36–38.

13. *Politica*, 1.2 (1253a), trans. Benjamin Jowett, in *The Works of Aristotle*, ed. W. D. Ross (Oxford: Clarendon Press, 1921), vol. 10.

14. "The Argument of Comedy," *English Institute Essays, 1948* (New York: Columbia University Press, 1949), p. 58.

15. But see Herford and Simpson, 1:279.

16. *The Cankered Muse*, pp. 190–191.

Index

Index

Fair, 136; on *A Tale of a Tub*, 162; on *Volpone*, 60

Knights, L. C.: on *Volpone*, 186n

Levin, Harry: on the satiric expositor in Jonson, 182n, 183n; on Subtle in *The Alchemist*, 120; on *Volpone*, 92–93, 185n

Levin, Richard: on *Bartholomew Fair*, 136, 189n, 190n

Machiavel: Dauphine as, 109

Mares, F. H.: on *The Alchemist*, 188n

Marlowe, Christopher: his version of Ovid's *Amores* used in *Poetaster*, 40

Menippean satire, 13–14, 57

Morris, Elisabeth Woodbridge: on *The Alchemist*, 115

Nash, Ralph: *Volpone* as comedy, 184n

Napoleon: Dauphine compared to, 109

Ornstein, Robert: on Jonson's pessimism, 4

Partridge, Edward: on *The Alchemist*, 115–116; on Jonson's development, 3; on *Volpone*, 60, 185n

Poetaster: analysis of, 39–54; "Apologetical Dialogue," 12, 56–57

Praz, Mario: on Jonson's depiction of Venice, 184n

Robinson, James: on *Bartholomew Fair*, 136

Rubens: Jonson compared to, 91

Sejanus, 56–57, 184n, 185n

Shakespeare, William: *Antony and Cleopatra*, 11; *Comedy of Errors*, 108, 165; *Cymbeline*, 154, 179; *King Lear*, 11, 58; *Macbeth*, 11; *Measure for Measure*, 154; *Merchant of Venice*, 100; *Merry Wives of Windsor*, 100; *Othello*, 156; *Pericles*, 11; *Tempest*, 156, 189n; *Twelfth Night*, 156

Sidney, Sir Philip, 42

Silent Woman. See Epicene

Simpson, Percy. *See* Herford, C. H.

Snell, Florence May: on *A Tale of a Tub*, 163

Steane, J. B.: on *The Alchemist*, 117, 120

Tale of a Tub: analysis of the play, 162–176

Talbert, Ernest William: on *Cynthia's Revels*, 183n

Thayer, Calvin: on *Bartholomew Fair*, 189n; on *Every Man out of His Humor*, 183n; on Jonson's humors, 181–182; on *Volpone*, 185n, 186n

Townsend, Freda: on *The Alchemist*, 189n; on *Bartholomew Fair*, 136; on *A Tale of a Tub*, 163

Virgil, 10

Volpone: analysis of, 56–91; Epistle Dedicatory to, 10–12, 93

Waith, Eugene M.: on *Bartholomew Fair*, 189n; on *Poetaster*, 184n

Weld, John S.: on *Volpone*, 186n

Wilson, Edmund: on Jonson as expressionist, 22

Zweig, Stefan: his adaptation of *Volpone*, 60, 185n